REMARKABLE BOOKS
about
YOUNG PEOPLE
with
SPECIAL NEEDS

Huron Street Press proceeds support the American Library Association in its mission to provide leadership for the development, promotion, and improvement of library and information services and the profession of librarianship in order to enhance learning and ensure access to information for all.

REMARKABLE BOOKS
about
YOUNG PEOPLE
with
SPECIAL NEEDS

ALISON M. G. FOLLOS

an imprint of the American Library Association

HURON STREET PRESS

CHICAGO • 2013

Alison Follos is the author of *Reviving Reading: School Library Programming, Author Visits, and Books That Rock!* (Neal-Schuman, 2006), which offers school librarians ideas for promoting creative literature programs—from integrating contemporary literature into the English curriculum to promoting reading for pleasure throughout the school. A school librarian for more than twenty years, Follos has presented reading incentive and read-aloud workshops for library professionals and educators throughout New York and New England, and at the 2007 American Library Association Annual Conference. In 2009 she cochaired the author committee for the American Association of School Librarians National Conference.

Printed in the United States of America

17 16 15 14 13   5 4 3 2 1

Extensive effort has gone into ensuring the reliability of the information in this book; however, the publisher makes no warranty, express or implied, with respect to the material contained herein.

ISBNs: 978-1-937589-13-4 (paper); 978-1-937589-29-5 (PDF); 978-1-937589-54-7 (ePub); 978-1-937589-55-4 (Kindle). For more information on digital formats, visit the ALA Store at alastore.ala.org and select eEditions.

Library of Congress Cataloging-in-Publication Data
Follos, Alison M. G.
  Remarkable books about young people with special needs / Alison M.G. Follos.
    pages   cm
  Includes bibliographical references and index.
  ISBN 978-1-937589-13-4 (pbk.)
  1. Children with disabilities—Books and reading. 2. Teenagers with disabilities—Books and reading. 3. Children with disabilities—Juvenile literature—Bibliography. 4. People with disabilities—Bibliography. 5. Children's literature, American—Bibliography. 6. Young adult literature, American—Bibliography. I. Title.
  Z1039.D5F65 2013
  028.5—dc23
                                                              2012023344

Composition by Casey Bayer using ITC Esprit and Geometric.
Cover design by Kim Thornton. Images © Shutterstock, Inc.

♾ This paper meets the requirements of ANSI/NISO Z39.48-1992 (Permanence of Paper).

To Holli and Elisa

for speaking up and choosing to be seen

Contents

Introduction

I am a middle school librarian who has worked with children and teens for 23 years. Within one book there is not enough room to cover the expansive range of learning disabilities, physical disabilities, medical illness, accident trauma, and emotional and psychological disorders that fall under the crowded umbrella term of *special needs*—but I'm going to give it a good shot! Included here are stories about children and young adults contending with a vast array of personal differences while striving to live vital lives. Sometimes the story is about a private challenge; other times, coping with external factors. Stories support counselors, ramps, aides, handicap facilities, and psychological and medical institutions. Stories help dissipate the discomfort of acknowledging special needs individuals and celebrate their remarkable daily accomplishments. Stories focus on a character's *character* instead of a character's disability.

Students talk about the books they love. They are unself-conscious about their recommendations, gushing over titles from Rick Riordan's wildly popular Percy Jackson and the Olympians series to Laurie Halse Anderson's fascinating—if disturbing—*Wintergirls*. Some teens say it quietly, by the types of books that they repeatedly choose. Others say it with loud enthusiasm as they shove title recommendations into a friend's hands. These titles take on a life of their own, circulating again and again. Often they are great books about tough times. Parents call my attention to titles they find particularly compelling, or, uncomfortably alarming. It might be a book that affected them profoundly by recalling their own family's circumstance. Or it is may be the realistic story of scary teen self-destructive behavior.

The novels and memoirs in this book have a special needs character at their heart. The stories are told through a young person's narrative or from a family member's viewpoint. Stories reveal experiences that we may not know about, but for the knowing, we become more compassionate. For those of us who identify with the character's challenge, these stories hearten our way. It is my pleasure to call these remarkable novels about remarkable characters to your attention.

What Books Are Recommended?

There are many page-turners about bad situations gone right—people who are born with a disability, or dealt a tough blow, yet persevere with tenacity, hope, dignity, discipline, and often times, with humor. Humor is a powerful tonic. The characters within these stories aren't defined by their special needs. They are memorable individuals with spunk and big personalities. Not all the stories are warm and fuzzy, and some are difficult to accept, but they all offer credibility and resolution. These stories make a connection with those afflicted—and raise awareness, provide inspiration, and garner support from those who think they aren't.

There are stories here about people who have battled obstacles: physical devastation from accidents, illness, social stigma from their differences, emotional depression, hidden family dysfunctions, shame, and an innumerable amount of other personal adversities. Knowing stories about survivors is fuel for survival. These stories offer support for the individual and for families, and they celebrate the extraordinary daily effort, determination, and ultimate success that accompany the struggle.

You'll find recommended books that celebrate character—great stories with unexploited lifetime drama, and sometimes even melodrama. Reading about Scott Hamilton or the late Terry Fox has little to do with the disease that marked them and everything to do with who they are and were. For the individual who is notably different from her peers, be it physically, emotionally, intellectually, or psychologically, that person has grit to persevere toward her goals. Perhaps her biggest challenge is to live within the conventional norm. As parents, neighbors, caregivers, friends, educators, and community members, we can share their remarkable stories and change perceptions.

There are also stories about perfectly normal and well-adjusted characters who have a family member or a friend who is dependent upon them and the demands and challenges that that situation presents. You'll find these novels in a section devoted to family members.

In most chapters there are recommendations of highly readable and popular page-turners for kids—books that encourage the pleasure of recreational reading. My professional belief is that reading aloud is good for teens—it is all-inclusive—so there is a section on titles that work well when read out loud.

Today there are contemporary, high-quality books being published that deserve great attention. Novels that feature vital, engaging characters who navigate through the pitfalls of the seemingly innocuous homogenized classroom to those who tackle the many challenges in the special education classroom. These resolute characters deal with learning disabilities, mental illness, emotional disorder, psychological trauma, a debilitating accident, or a life-threatening medical condition and keep on going. You learn an awful lot from people through reading about their lives. Stories inspire us to persevere against personal adversity and acknowledge and honor the differences around us.

Not all readers will enjoy all the recommended titles in this book. There are times when we need to escape our discomfort, not come face to face with it. For instance, children with Asperger's syndrome might be uncomfortable reading about anyone who is teased or picked on; who is sad, under emotional duress or experiencing high anxiety; or who is having trouble contending with their differences. Such stories may exacerbate their already heightened and sensitive temperaments. For these readers, we've included title recommendations from people who have dealt with similar struggles. For those of us who don't know what living with Asperger's is like, or what living with a person who has Asperger's is like, novels that reveal the experience make inroads to help us understand.

Isn't Life Ironic?

Our children are overfed on tabloid stories of athletic heroics—from endurance to excess. In a culture that prizes winning above all else, that values success above happiness, we have created an inevitably high bar for certain failure and disappointment. Small accomplishments are deemed insignificant. Consider our obsession with extreme sports: young athletes push beyond safe physical limits; they are lured away from their education with inappropriate salaries that supersede all common sense; being an Olympic contender is inconsequential if the athlete doesn't medal; if an athlete doesn't nab the gold medal their stats are briefly boasted on a cereal box before their achievement fades into obscurity. The gross expectation of winning obliterates the base gratification of physical well-being and contentment. Pierre de Coubertin, founder of the modern Olympic Games, said, "The most important thing in the Olympic Games is not to win but to take part, just as the most important thing in life is not the triumph but the struggle."[1]

In the novels recommended in this book you'll discover winners from among those often perceived as losers. *Remarkable Books about Young People with Special Needs* promotes stories about the extraordinary daily effort of living in a "normal"-peopled world. The trick is reaching deep and finding the inner resolve to try and thus triumph. Stories of survival against the odds hold allure and motivation for all readers. Here are stories about seemingly impossible successes against seemingly insurmountable odds. Such stories can be influential—even pivotal—and may make a difference between trying and withdrawing. We encourage you to read some of them and embrace the struggle.

Good books about tough stuff breach avoidance and bring people together. There is safety within familiarity. In a story you walk with a stranger exploring unfamiliar and uncomfortable turf. In a "normal" kid's daily life, a special needs classmate may be considered peculiar—if they are considered at all. It takes a story to develop awareness, to encourage tolerance and acceptance. What makes Joey lose control may have little to do with his intent and much to do with something else. A story takes that something else and makes it tangible.

You'll find a bank of novels reviewed in each chapter—novels like Sharon Draper's *Out of My Mind,* about 11-year-old Melody who has cerebral palsy (CP) and has never spoken a word. Words dance silently in her head; she plays with them, organizes them, and fits them together. Unable to speak her brilliant mind, her ideas are frustratingly locked inside. When Melody learns to use an electronic keyboard device, she is at long last able to "talk." But of course the simple act of communicating does not make for a completely happy ending. Melody's grit as she picks herself up from social disappointments and focuses on her next goal is the spine of the story. She accomplishes the hitherto unimaginable: transforming herself from quietly disabled to outspoken.

What's Your Secret?

In my own family there are secrets, from alcohol and substance abuse, depression, eating disorders, physical disabilities, anxiety, panic attacks, denial, and so on. We avoid talking about our family's vulnerabilities among one another and hide them from the public. The outward signs may be subtle or hidden, but dysfunction, disorders, and disabilities seem to be a natural part of life. There are many recommended novels that reveal families living with special needs. Such family situations are more common than we realize.

Remarkable Books about Young People with Special Needs shares the adventure of personal challenge. No matter how insurmountable the obstacle, these stories present support through family and friends, and acceptance. Books aren't shy. They are candid, honest, and intimate. They ring true and nudge us past our daily grind. Stories stir the secrets that we bury, and they don't judge us. The power of literature is sneaky. On the page are the words and ideas that stir memories moldering deep under cover of denial. Someone else had a fear, an ugly thought, an irrational behavior, a time so dark and seemingly hopeless, so why bother? But in taking the time, by making the effort to read a story, you may discover more than you bargained for. You may accept your foibles and become more tolerant of others' needs. Stories are a realistic way to face the unimaginable.

How Educators Help

Special needs children are often pulled from mainstream classes. Although this practice may provide special instruction and care, it reduces the interaction and exchange that children benefit from while being in the mainstream. Stories share and dispel the mystery of what goes on in other people's lives. In a perfect world, a book might change a person's perspective, develop awareness, and initiate conversation to knock down walls and bridge the gap between misfortune and misconception.

Books that tackle psychological battles that teens deal with such as eating disorders, cutting, depression, or suicide offer up opportunity for discussion. Many teens are more interested in these topics than they'll admit (or than their parents are aware). School library circulation figures show that stories dealing with edgy, controversial subject matter are checked out regularly and frequently. Bookstores show that similar teen reads are the brunt of their young adult book sales. It is not unusual for stories about cutting and anorexia to be checked out by 10-year-old girls. Tweens are curious. Using such a book in a group setting—perhaps a read-aloud, literary circle, or book club with teens—offers opportunity for discussion. You might invite the school counselor to participate and help process the conversation that such books will instigate. One such story was James Howe's *Totally Joe* (Atheneum Books for Young Readers, 2007), a book about a 12-year-old dealing with the myriad of social conflicts, confrontations, and explanations of being openly gay in middle school. One student who read it said, "That was really unusual. I've never read a story like this," and after a pause he added, "I never really thought about that."

Independence Is a Tricky Word

As a special needs individual you may be dependent upon other people in unexpected ways. This is to say, personal goals will be contingent upon assistance, and privacy may be limited. While rehab, instruction, and encouragement are part of a quest toward self-sufficiency, the fact is that if you are physically disabled, achieving complete independence will be difficult—perhaps impossible. Stories about people who achieve small and huge steps toward independence are real and inspirational. One is the renowned Helen Keller, who fought her way beyond her visual and auditory disabilities to live a vibrant and accomplished life (*Helen Keller: Rebellious Spirit*). Another is the famous Olympian Scott Hamilton, who overcame a childhood illness to become greater than the great odds stacked against him (*The Great 8: How to Be Happy Even When You Have Every Reason to Be Miserable*). Stories about ordinary kids like 5-year-old Cory Friedman who woke up one day seemingly possessed, his nervous system wracked by the mysterious assault of Tourette's syndrome (*Med Head*). You'll meet Elisa and her mother, Holli, real people in my upstate New York town. They generously agreed to several interviews for this book. They share anecdotes of the difficult chapters in their daily lives. By doing so, Elisa and Holli risk being visible and vulnerable—because they believe that literature raises awareness.

This book is for the rest of us to learn about what it's like for the rest of us. We are all as different and individual as our fingerprints, yet we are often most comfortable with those whose prints resemble our own. In reading stories about people who tackle life head on every day because life is harder for them, we venture outside our comfort zone. We discover that people's differences can be more interesting, perhaps even more exciting, than our similarities. Sharing their stories is a beginning. For the person who is lucky enough to be born without a disability; lucky enough not to deal with family trauma, dysfunction, or mental illness; lucky to be spared medical illness, a learning disability, or accidental injury—for that individual these stories share the valor of survival, the triumph over adversity. For others less fortunate, recognizing differences through story won't cure what disturbs, unsettles, or challenges their very core, but shared stories move us past isolation, a sense of helpless misfortune, or self-imposed limits.

Within the following chapters are book recommendations about people who work very hard to never give up. If you fit the definition of *normal*, or if you don't, you'll be hard pressed not to be affected by these stories. My mission is to get these stories to your children, grandchildren, caregivers, friends, students, and families. To everyone who is too busy, too uncomfortable, too afraid, or too unaware of the benefits of acknowledging our differences. These stories are not about special needs; they are about remarkable people.

NOTE

1. Pierre de Coubertin, borrowed from the speech of Bishop Ethelbert Talbot at a service for Olympic champions during the 1908 Olympic Games, quoted at http://history1900s.about .com/od/greateventsofthecentury/a/olympicfacts.htm.

one

The Value of Reading for All

For Escape, Motivation, or Empowerment

Why Would a "Normal" Kid Read a Book about a Special Needs Kid?

The gist of this book is recommending stories that have merit for any reader, whether it be through personal identity, empathy, escape, intellectual satisfaction, or personal growth. As a children's and young adult school librarian I have witnessed the most unlikely readers enjoying the most unlikely books. For instance, there's a sixth-grade boy who is so impulsively active that adults trail him, throwing out cautious "be careful"s. He is so physically rambunctious that it is not uncommon to see one or another of his limbs swaddled in a sling or covered in a cast. His favorite books are anything that Rick Riordan writes: action, myth, special powers, and adventure. One day he asked if I had *Rules*, the story of a young girl with an autistic little brother. It was a surprising request from such a lively and impetuous young boy. When he returned the book I asked him how he liked it. He said, "I don't usually read this kind of book, but it was different and I liked it. My best friend's older brother is like the kid in the book. He's 21 and he just moved into a special home. But when he's home, we let him play with us. He's nice. Yeah, I liked this book." Children and young adults enjoy well-written stories that share different lifestyles and experiences. The reality is that *normal* is a fluid and subjective concept defined by friends, family lifestyle, and personal perspective.

When I recommend books to children, the intention is to offer books that they will like—for pleasure, relaxation, and joy. Stories are a positive alternative universe to the reality some of us contend with. No doubt that is exactly why many kids select fantasy and mythology tales. Lands that enable the frail to be strong, the powerless to be powerful, the disadvantaged to be infused with good fortune, the insecure and timid to be audacious and courageous—in short, the ability to transform from what we are into what we wish to be. Stories offer a moment of reprieve from the daily grind, and in some cases, the struggle. Books exercise the imagination.

What do children want from a story? Many want to escape. They want to become superheroes, or fall into perfect ending romances, or laugh over nonsense. A good book helps transport them away from restrictions. The pressures of daily life, the *booorrring* school demands, or in the case of children with special needs, release from their day-to-day challenges. Recently a mother told me that her intellectually inclined and physically talented child read thirty books over the summer. She read titles like the Trixie Belden series, *The Borrowers, Homer Price.* Why is she reading the books of the '50s? Her mother answered, "Because she likes happy endings. She doesn't want to read anything mean or dark." If a child with high intellectual abilities and strong athletic capabilities wants "happy endings" from her stories, we can assume that children facing daily adversities do too.

Another parent shared that her physically, emotionally, and mentally challenged child loves stories but that after trying to read a paragraph independently, she's exhausted and falling asleep. Her reading teacher has her reading Hemingway's *The Old Man and the Sea,* Rawls's *Where the Red Fern Grows,* Steinbeck's *The Red Pony*, and other classic titles. Many children don't like what is considered classic literature. Olympic figure skater Scott Hamilton, who is a cancer survivor and living with a brain tumor, told me, "When I was a kid I didn't like the classics. Now I appreciate the genius of classic literature. But I still don't really enjoy reading them."[1] (There's a lot of truth to Mark Twain's quote "A classic is something that everybody wants to have read and nobody wants to read."[2]) Literature appreciation is kind of like being at an art museum; kids rush pell-mell through the galleries, hiding in the maze of nooks and crannies. It takes a lot of years and cultural exposure before they stop to admire the artwork. Reading must be enjoyable for a kid to invest the work involved in learning *how* to read. To be a strong reader requires practice. Enticing stories keep kids reading. As with any art, a reader has a lifetime to appreciate the finer aspects of literature.

The stories recommended throughout this book zoom in on the central theme of living with, or overcoming, adversity. Stories that make the unbelievable believable. In a culture that encourages us to juggle a daily fix of leisure, personal pleasures, athletics, multiple communications, professional responsibilities, and family and household demands, we tend to shy away from personal difficulties and handicaps. Yet life throws zingers at everyone. No one is immune. Many people face a physical disability, a learning disability, a psychological affliction, a dependency, or an emotional challenge. Many special needs individuals live isolated by their differences. The odd thing is that special needs affect so many of our lives, yet so many of us fail to acknowledge or accept this. We are reluctant to share our family tales, face our personal challenges, or accept one another's special needs, anomalies, idiosyncrasies, oddities, abnormalities, afflictions, addictions, adversities— or whatever other descriptive label you may choose. We experience discomfort when confronting differences. Novels and stories don't. They speak with candor and courage. They bridge the gap, reveal a secret, dissolve guarded isolation, push back the stigma, and remove well-intentioned barriers. While stories open windows and bridge divides, they also incite compassion, tolerance, and awareness.

Children's and young adult author Jerry Spinelli consistently presents stories that pit unusual, sometimes quixotic characters against conflicts within stereotypical conformity. For all his characters, from ordinary to exceptional, Spinelli's novels spin the stuff that children *get*. Spinelli infuses ordinary settings with power; he coaxes forth the strength and respect of the natural environment and the innate natural potential of the individual. He explores the contemporary version of an old theme: the social quandary of being different. Take his guileless hero, the orphan in *Maniac Magee*. Maniac is trying to survive in a segregated township. He runs through the streets like a phantom child and lives in a zoo, caring for and being cared for. At every turn Maniac has social, ethical, and racial obstacles to surmount—until somewhere along the story line, the young character emerges victorious, larger than life, pumping up the reader with the positive possibilities of independent, dignified, and honorable behavior.

Because of Spinelli's consistent representation of nonconforming characters thriving in and, more often than not, affecting their flawed status quo surroundings, I approached him about contributing to this book. I was particularly interested in his book *Loser*, in which the main character, Donald Zinkoff—known throughout the story as Zinkoff—is slower than the norm in many areas. I wrote to Spinelli, describing Zinkoff as a mentally challenged character. Spinelli replied,

> I personally do not see Zinkoff as *challenged* as we seem to use the term today. Among the duller tacks in the box? Yes. Clumsy? Yes. Bad speller? Yes. Slow afoot? Yes. But he is, in even the other kids' eyes, a "loser," not an idiot or moron or whatever unkind term kids might use for such a person. In my view Zinkoff is not defective; he just doesn't score very high on common yardsticks. I do understand that some readers perceive Zinkoff as mentally challenged, and I long ago transferred interpretation rights to my readers—but I just don't think I can present a view that does not line up with my original intention.[3]

Spinelli also wrote about the deep well from which Zinkoff springs and the profound effect he has on readers.

> Sports kid that I was, my favorite poem in those growing-up days was by the legendary Grantland Rice:
>
> > When the One Great Scorer comes
> > To mark against your name,
> > He writes—not what you won or lost—
> > But how you played the Game.
>
> Except for the winning-isn't-everything-it's-the-only-thing crowd, few would disagree with the wisdom of that sentiment. Few, also, are those who seem to live by it. We are a culture that covets first place—"We're No. 1!"—and we don't much care how we get there. Winners, we love them. We want to be them. Because if you're not a winner, well then, you must be a loser. What else is there?
>
> Into this cultural minefield staggers Zinkoff. In his school, among his peers, Zinkoff is called a "loser." Why? Because he comes up short on commonly recognized measures for excellence: grades, footspeed, coordination, social grace. In the unarticulated dynamic of the school, having a "loser" around is good, even necessary, so others can feel like winners.
>
> And so the scoreboard would read forever—Others: 1, Zinkoff: 0—except for one thing: losing requires the cooperation of the "loser." And Zinkoff doesn't know he's a loser. Not that he thinks he's a winner either. He doesn't think either way. He doesn't see the world as Losers and Winners. All he sees is people. He doesn't take the measure of others. Or himself. He doesn't keep score. All he does is play the Game. Joyously. Honestly. Until in the end, others begin to notice—and put away their scorecards.[4]

With Jerry Spinelli's championing of Zinkoff we are a little wiser. Such a story is the stuff that inspires children to pause and think beyond their pack mentality. It prods readers to recognize those who participate in life with wholehearted enthusiasm, without the need for approval and without an ulterior quest for reward.

It is refreshing to read stories about the accomplishments of ordinary individuals in the face of extraordinary challenges. Realistic stories that are absent of greed and filled with success. A story about a paralyzed victim whose extreme accomplishment, after months of rehab therapy, is feeding herself with a special spork; the older teen who will never have his driver's license (unlike his younger 16-year-old brother), but looks forward to holding a job and living in a group home; a teen who hides her self-destructive behaviors until she's brave enough to ask for help—all these stories are seriously inspiring. Special needs individuals have meaningful life goals: to achieve independence, to communicate with their family and others, to have careers and form friendships. Having such stories available and calling them to our readers' attention is of significant service for all. Stories help keep personal unrealistic expectations in perspective and are an integral step to erase the separation factor. We *are* affected by each other's needs, directly or through association. We may even be tethered, reassured, and awakened by them.

Why Would a Special Needs Kid Read about Special Needs?

Recently a parent of a visually impaired child said, "I remember when my son read Michael Dorris's book *Sees behind Trees*. He was so excited. He said, 'Mom he's just like me! I have trouble seeing, but I can hear better than anybody.'" The book is a coming-of-age tale about a nearsighted Native American boy. The boy's other senses are heightened and compensate for his vision disability. He gains confidence in himself and earns the respect of his tribe when he escorts an elderly wise man on a dangerous journey. Their son's connection with the boy in the novel was a heartening moment for the whole family.

Another child wrote about her excitement over author Marlee Matlin's novel *Deaf Child Crossing*. This girl had worn two hearing aids since she was 2 years old. She spoke of identifying with Matlin's book because there is a girl "with the same problem as me— two hearing aids and kids that tease her." She was relieved that there was a story about a girl with hearing aids and ran to the library to check it out. She said, "I was touched that an author would bother to write a book about such a thing."

In addition to stories offering fantasy and escape, there is connection with characters of similar or different challenges—the human connection that dispels the loneliness.

Stories encourage individuals to see life in unexpected ways, through experiences that may otherwise be impossible to imagine. Trapped in a physically uncooperative body, a child watches other children climb and play. In a story, she goes along. She is part of the group. Her imagination lets her ride piggyback on the story; all she needs to do to participate is to show up. Stories have the stuff that takes you places—despite real life limits.

How to Get Kids Reading

To the parent who frets over the quality of what his child is reading, or to the English teacher who feels the need to "challenge" her students with high analytical literary content, my commonsense argument is this: if we're to motivate children to read, we must give them things they'll want to read. Reading is fun. Parents frustrated by what their child reads tell me in exasperation, "He will read if it's what he likes." That makes sense. Adults about to relax and watch television after a day of work choose to be entertained by something particular to their recreational inclinations. Typically their first choice is not a program on nuclear physics—or it may be, but it is *their* choice. For leisure reading we don't usually reach for our insurance policy. Most children who plant themselves in front of the TV don't watch CNN or the Weather Channel. If they were assigned, or allowed, to watch only those programs, they may not watch TV. They watch the fun stuff. Getting a child to love reading means providing material that she'll enjoy reading: comics, magazines, love stories, horror, mystery—anything and everything that will hold her interest and attention and entertain her. Let children experience the pleasure of reading. If the text is overwhelming or of little interest and the content difficult to comprehend, chances are the reader will put down the book. Becoming comfortable with literature begins slowly: sitting quietly, turning the pages (or listening to a read-aloud), imagining the story as it unfolds. If your child is interested in nuclear physics, find books and magazines to fuel that. Magazines like *Popular Science* and *Discover* are great choices. If he is interested in superheroes, find the comics that will be sure to entertain him. The more children love to read, the more they'll choose to read.

Of fundamental importance is finding the right material to match individual readers' tastes. That's when the assistance of a librarian is a valuable resource. I do not pretend to have a background in the clinical world of special needs individuals, but I do have extensive knowledge about children's and young adult literature. This extends to experience with children and young adults, learning about their likes and dislikes, which in turn influences their literary tastes. Sometimes I love titles that my students hate, and vice versa. Librarians are aware of what teen readers gravitate toward, which often is far different from what we like or what the award committees say children and teens should like. Too often the award winners sit dusty on the shelves.

A parent of a child suffering from emotional stress shook his head in disappointment before sharing, "He'll only read fantasy. He reads the Brian Jacques books over and over again." I could sense the father's torment but in fact, Brian Jacques's Redwall series is well loved, and his books are read over and over again by bright and successful students. There's absolutely nothing wrong with reading the same loved story over and over again. I had a student who I was unable to budge past reading anything outside of the Redwall realm. She frustrated me with her steadfast attraction. She grew up, came back to work at school, and is a delightful, creative, and productive employee. She loves to read—everything.

We have numerous volumes of Jeff Smith's Bone series in the library. We've replaced several of these titles several times due to frequent circulation. They fall apart because they're read so often. Encourage students to read whatever they like, because reading is too important to be shamed into a guilty pleasure.

Another place to help children and teens find appealing reading material is the local bookstore. Privately owned bookstores usually have shopkeepers who know the market and the most current commercial hits. Your library may not have the "book dumps" with all the newest marketing gimmicks—books that are out before the movie, books that mimic the movie, rereleases of books with new covers because of the movie. The fad factor and commercialism may turn you off, but we're looking to turn kids on to books here. Commercialism seeps into every aspect of our culture; use it when it works for a good cause. Magazines are a huge attraction to teens. Ironically parents fret over their nonreading children who pore over a fashion, news, sports, or graphic magazine for hours. A popular book for many students, including those with reading disabilities, is the *Guinness Book of World Records*. For whatever content you may wish to pass by yourself, don't ignore the fact that children and teens are sitting, absorbing, turning pages, reading, and exclaiming over whatever freakish absurdities they discover on the page. This is the beginning of a great thing.

NOTES

1. Scott Hamilton, interview with the author, Lake Placid, New York, November 27, 2010.

2. Mark Twain, attributed, November 20, 1900, www.quotationspage.com/quote/172.html.

3. Jerry Spinelli, e-mail to the author, January 12, 2010.

4. Ibid.

two

Books Aren't Shy—People Are

Special Needs Is Not an Embarrassment

It is not uncommon for those of us who perceive ourselves as "normal" to regard visibly special needs individuals with reservation, shyness, and awkwardness. We may avoid eye contact, conversation, or connection with a special needs person or their families. We may act uncomfortable with accident victims or people suffering from disease. This is no surprise, because when at all possible most of us downplay our own personal challenges. We go through our lives trying to control our personality quirks, mask our physical flaws, and hide our psychological vulnerabilities. In our quest for a perfect body and a perfect world, imperfections embarrass us. It is no wonder that if we at all acknowledge a medically, psychologically, or physically disabled individual, it is with tentative caution.

Easy to Be Invisible

When I interviewed Scott Hamilton, I was unaware that he was recovering from brain surgery—for the second time. It wasn't until he explained, in detail, his 10 surgeries within the past 6 months that I learned of the brain tumor discovered a few months earlier in 2010. Had I known about his recent surgery, I would have averted my attention and not imposed on his privacy. I would have lost the candid story of his struggle; a message of recovery that he feels deeply about sharing. He said, "I was given a great sense of opportunity to help others who struggle."[1]

Fifteen years ago a friend of my daughter's had a younger sibling who was diagnosed with *something*. Meeting the mom in the parking lot of the market, I cooed over her 10-month-old baby, Elisa. An odd expression crossed her face before she said, "Something isn't right. She should be sitting up independently by now. We're taking her to the Children's Hospital in Boston next week." I nodded dumbly, asked no more, got into my car, and drove away. Elisa may as well have been the invisible baby.

Over the years our families would gather at sporting events, and we would chat and compare notes about our children—our healthy, "normal" children. We didn't speak about what was wrong with Elisa, their beautiful growing daughter who had difficulty speaking and whose steps were unbalanced and halting. I dared not ask *the question*.

Elisa has cerebral palsy.

When researching for this book—after 15 years of living in the same community as Elisa and her family—I approached them to see if Elisa would be willing to talk about reading, books, and the impact (if any) stories make on her life. I was cautious, sensitive about their privacy and worried that they would be offended by my curiosity. Their response was a surprise. They were excited to have Elisa included in the project. Her mother, Holli, a speech-language pathologist, explained, "She's had a very difficult year. She's been pulled out of school for behavioral issues. She's having home tutoring about 6 hours a week, and we're supplementing that. It will be good for her to feel worthwhile. I explained to Elisa that this will be her opportunity to advocate for other special needs individuals and speak up for them."[2]

Meet Elisa

You will hear from Elisa and her parents in several sections of this book. To understand their perspectives, and where Elisa's coming from, you need to know a little bit about her. The following entries are from 3 visits over the course of a year.[3]

July 2010

At 15 years old, Elisa reads at a second-grade level. Her comprehension is on par with her grade, but reading independently at grade level is overwhelming. Exhausting. Her mother reads to her. While her peer group negotiates the public school social scene, Elisa is often alone, working from home. Most of her interactions are with adults: tutors, horseback riding instructors, physical therapists, her parents, and her three older brothers. While at school she is affected by what goes on around her. "She is so in tune with what everyone else is doing, but she can't do it," explains her mom. For Elisa, the opportunity to experience the world through literature is limited because of her limited independent reading skills.

Elisa's cerebral palsy is complicated by other psychological disabilities that have yet to be accurately diagnosed. "Elisa has difficulty reading on her own because of her visual perception," Holli says. "It's like she's looking through a keyhole, and everything on the periphery is blurry. That's how the doctor explained it. She gets very tired trying to read independently, so I read aloud to her."

Her current psychological consultants have tried a battery of medications, including most recently birth control to try and regulate the mood swings brought on by her menstrual cycle. Unfortunately one medication seems to counteract another, and a successful balance is still to be found.

Her mother describes Elisa's "meltdowns": when Elisa's stress and anxiety level build up, she explodes—clears tables, screams, kicks, and is barely able to be restrained. She is unable to fall asleep without her mother wrapping her arms tightly about her and throwing a leg over her legs, "like a cocoon." Blankets, surrounding pillows—nothing replaces the comfort that she receives from her mother's weight. When they consider alternative boarding schools or residential homes for Elisa, you can see the anxiety in Holli's eyes. "I don't know how she'll ever fall asleep," she says. "They'll have to sedate her." For a family who values their time together, who places emphasis on the benefits of staying physically healthy, who wants their daughter to live at home, who are facing the selfless reality of what is best for her, and who avoid medicating her as much as possible, sedating Elisa is a distressing option.

During summer school, Elisa works on her independent reading skills. When Elisa tries to read on her own it is extraordinarily difficult for her. She suffers from her visual peripheral impairment. Holli explains, "After one paragraph she is exhausted. It is a tremendous amount of eyestrain for her to focus on the letters." I wondered what she was reading in her summer school program. "This year they have read, or started reading, *Of Mice and Men* [by John Steinbeck]—which she read last year—and recently, *The Pigman* [by Paul Zindel]. I'm not trying to be difficult, but these are not great choices for Elisa. In my opinion, *The Pigman* is a dark story; a man's wife dies, he goes into the hospital, kids destroy his apartment, and then in the end, he dies. For a child who is dealing with depression and is hypersensitive, a story like this is overwhelming. Now they're reading a Gary Paulsen novel about dogs and Alaska. They've changed books three times this fall! But Elisa doesn't seem to care." It is evident that Holli does care.

People with differences and disabilities must work hard. Traits like gumption, tenacity, and perseverance make up their daily arsenal. Yet they aren't always able to forge ahead as independently as they'd like. As was the case in the book *Out of My Mind*, when the main character, who also had CP, depended on her mother, her neighbor, and the student aide to advocate on her behalf and put things within her reach. Elisa liked *Out of My Mind*, though Holli says, "She's hypersensitive and when the girl was left behind on the trip to Washington, it definitely upset Elisa." What about the resolution at the end, where Melody is celebrated in the class? Holli shakes her head sadly because, for Elisa, that didn't make much of a difference.

This ends our summer interview, and I leave books behind for the next visit.

December 20, 2010

Today Elisa speaks about *Out of My Mind*. "It was interesting because even though Melody can't talk, we have some of the same thoughts. There are a lot of mean kids. She kind of is like me 'cause people don't realize what you can do. I have to show both the kids and the adults what I can do." Elisa, facing down a bit of her fear and sensitivity, is now focused on Melody's strength rather than concentrating on her disappointment.

What other books did Elisa like? "*Petey* was different. It showed what it was like to be a grownup with CP and how adults treat you. But [*Out of My Mind*] is different because I can relate and I liked reading about a girl who deals with so many of the things that I do. If you're a girl like me with CP and you are going to school, and you're going to graduate, you can understand all the obstacles that she is coping with."

I ask Elisa if she had had any time to read some of the books that I had brought last month. "I've been so busy. Every day of my life is not like other kids'; I have to jump through so many hoops every single day just to get through every day."

She turned toward her mom. "Today we had gym and I signed up for Ping-Pong." Holli is surprised, and they share a chuckle over Elisa's choice. "I played but I lost. I didn't care. I just like to play." She looks over at Holli. "May I go out now?" Elisa has clearly lost interest in our conversation. It's a lot of effort for her to talk, and still more work for her to help me understand all her thoughts. Often she must repeat herself, or look toward her mother to clear things up. As she told me, her day is filled with having to jump through many hoops, hoops that the rest of us take for granted. An ordinary afternoon conversation takes a lot of work for Elisa to be understood. The only thing I'm finding easy about Elisa is an understanding of her intense frustration level.

Elisa's enthusiasm over playing Ping-Pong reminds me of Jerry Spinelli's description of his protagonist Zinkoff: "And Zinkoff doesn't know he's a loser. Not that he thinks he's a winner either. He doesn't think either way. He doesn't see the world as Losers and Winners. All he sees is people. He doesn't take the measure of others. Or himself. He doesn't keep score. All he does is play the Game. Joyously. Honestly. Until in the end, others begin to notice—and put away their scorecards."[4]

June 25, 2011

Elisa looks tired today. Initially she answers my questions with a shy and whispery "I don't know." She is hesitant to join the table and be involved in the discussion. Holding up a title I ask her, "Do you think that this would make a good classroom read?"

"I don't know." Shy smile.

"What book did you like the most?"

Faraway thoughtful gaze, then bashful head-tucked-into-shoulder shrug, shy smile. "I don't know." She slowly moves away from the table and disappears upstairs.

Later on, after I visited with Holli for a while, Elisa comes back and is more engaged. "I liked *Running Dream* because she never gave up. Her friends kept encouraging her to run again. I liked it. She was nervous about going back to school. It was good to show that she could do it."

I ask Elisa if she feels it is important for kids to read books about people who have disabilities. "Yeah, because I don't think they can understand what it's like to be put in my body. Everybody tells me that they know what I'm going through, but they don't know what it's like. They don't really understand. They will get kind of a better idea when they read about these kids. It might make them think about it." Does she like reading about other teens in challenging situations? "Yes. It lets me know that I'm not the only one having a tough time. These kinds of books make me feel less alone."

Elisa hasn't had the experience of talking about the books she's read with a group of peers. She describes her special education class: "There are three other boys in my class. All of them have been in handcuffs. One is a father. They all have parole officers. They swear and make fun of everything. They punch the wall. They punch the door. We don't have conversations about books because they make fun of everything. Most of my day I spend crying. I love school, but I don't know if I can take another year with these boys."

Holli shakes her head in exasperation. "We have spoken to the school about making adaptations to the mainstream classes so that Elisa may attend, but this doesn't seem to happen. They try to do one thing, and then that day Elisa's behavior makes it impossible for her to participate. So that's frustrating. Now she's lost an entire year—tenth grade—of being in any of the core mainstream classes, so I'm not sure she would be able to catch up and enter the eleventh grade."

This year Elisa has read *The Old Man and the Sea* by Hemingway, *To Kill a Mockingbird* by Harper Lee, and *A Separate Peace* by John Knowles. She liked *To Kill A Mockingbird,* which she was required to read twice in two different classes, and she hated *The Old Man and the Sea.* Holli wonders, "Why can't they read books that have to do with other teens? Well-written novels about teens who are dealing with adversity? This might be an eye-opener for the rest of the students."

Holli's question echoes in my mind. What kind of a reading experience would Elisa have if she studied books about characters that she identifies with? What if she were in a class that talked about the stories that they read? Would that make her solitary world larger? Would she feel more connected? Would she make friends?

Author Sharon Draper writes about Melody, the main character who has cerebral palsy in her novel *Out of My Mind*, "I suppose the character of Melody came from my experiences in raising a child with developmental difficulties. But Melody is not my daughter . . . I was fiercely adamant that nobody feel sorry for Melody. I wanted her to be accepted as a character and as a person, not as a representative for people with disabilities. Melody is a tribute to all the parents of disabled kids who struggle, to all those children who are misunderstood, to all those caregivers who help every step of the way. It's also written for people who look away, who pretend they don't see, or who don't know what to say when they encounter someone who faces life with obvious differences. Just smile and say hello!"[5]

Holli tells it this way: "Elisa knows that she can't do everything that other girls do. Her cousins are her same age; they are valedictorians, honor students, they model, they're athletic. When they visit and everyone is outside sledding, or doing things, Elisa often stays in our room. She may be difficult to understand, but she understands. One thing she hates is when people speak to her as though she's a baby.

"She came home the other day and told me, 'Do you know those boys in my class have all been to court?' She is definitely aware of being paired up with them. There was a fire drill at school yesterday and Elisa said that the special ed teacher came and took her away from the mainstream class to stand with that group of boys. She would love to be friends with girls her age, and she notices that she isn't. She told me, 'Sometimes I feel invisible.'"

Books and stories will not change Elisa's daily challenges, but they motivate and inspire her to push back. Stories may reduce her growing sense of isolation.

In order to have empathy and to understand the experiences of others, we must know their stories. Reading helps develop awareness by sharing sensitive situations. Stories can generate empathy and dissipate the tendency to avoid special needs individuals for fear or embarrassment. And stories help us tiptoe beyond our comfort zone. Laurie Halse Anderson said, "Books can be a mirror for your own conditions, or a window into somebody else's."[6] Writing this book faced me toward the window to meet Elisa and took me beyond my superficial reflection.

NOTES

1. Scott Hamilton, interview with the author, Lake Placid, New York, November 27, 2010.

2. Series of family interviews, upstate New York, 2010–2011.

3. Ibid.

4. Jerry Spinelli, e-mail to the author, January 12, 2010.

5. Sharon Draper, "Behind the Book: The Story behind *Out of My Mind*," Simon and Schuster, http://books.simonandschuster.com/Out-of-My-Mind/Sharon-M-Draper/9781416971719/ behind_the_book (last accessed August 7, 2012).

6. Laurie Halse Anderson, author visit, North Country School, Lake Placid, NY, 2010.

Stories That Break the Stigma

Learning Disabilities and Behavioral Differences
in the Family and in the Classroom

Aside from the obvious, there are subtleties associated with learning disabilities. Children with learning disabilities work harder to grasp the basic mechanics necessary to navigate through the core curriculum. Dyslexia, the visual mix-up of letters on the page, impacts every academic class a student takes—from textbooks, blackboards, whiteboards, and smartboards to homework sheets and independent reading. Due to the increased number of learning disability cases, the educational support systems are overloaded and services are stretched thin. Budget cuts compound the situation. Children and young adults may fall through the cracks with undiagnosed learning disabilities, from ADHD to dyslexia. Such cases often morph into behavior issues. Self-esteem takes a hit when a student tries to conceal his disability, using class clowning as a decoy or by overcompensating in other areas; family members may be unaware of their child's struggle or incapable of assessing the problem. Educators may be overwhelmed with crowded classroom demands; they're unable to give individual students the extra help that they need. Slight learning disabilities can be difficult to notice and easy to ignore but are no less complicated to live with. All learning disabilities disrupt a child's educational progress and are emotionally distressing.

One of my students wrote about how the book *Bud, Not Buddy*, by Christopher Paul Curtis, changed how he felt about reading. He was going through a rough period, coming to grips with the harsh reality that he had a reading disability and facing the fact that it was actually affecting him in many areas. He was frustrated because his teacher made him read every night and he hated the books that she assigned to him. Reading not only became harder but simultaneously more hateful. Somehow he stumbled upon *Bud, Not Buddy,* and it piqued his interest. He liked it! And so he began to read. He even began to like reading, which was a good feeling at a not-so-great-time in his life. Reading still took him more time and effort than the other kids, but it was no longer such a miserable and despicable task.

For the child with learning differences, books about other students who struggle—with similar issues or unrelated ones—offer motivation and extend acceptance. They encourage self-awareness, courage, and empowerment. It is typical for people coping with learning differences to feel overwhelmed and depressed. Exacerbating the problem is confusion. Why don't I get it? Why am I so dumb? Why do I hate school? Why am I depressed? They are out of sync with the rest of their class, and their class is often frustrated with them, the disruptions they cause, and the attention they demand. It is a fragile, frayed, and too frequent classroom scene. Finding titles that children and young adults like to read, and making them feel good about their choices, is a viable solution. It doesn't matter if we feel that they're reading "below their level." The fact is that they're *reading*, and if there are more books available to be enjoyed, they'll read more and gain confidence. They do so in a pleasurable manner without the stigma of being told their choices don't count, are irrelevant, are insignificant, or worst of all, are "beneath their level." That negative reaction serves to develop an ingrained self-conscious distaste for something we're desperate for children to embrace. Let them read what they like.

The Classroom Clash

Many children who are labeled with ADHD are initially tolerated as normal but active kids. It's when they are forced to sit still in their classroom chair that the trouble begins. The earlier we're able to get reading material into their lives that explains the difficult transitions they are experiencing, the better.

Laurie Halse Anderson explains her family's experience with ADHD:

> *The Hair of Zoe Fleefenbacher* is dedicated to my daughter Meredith because it is about her. She doesn't have wild, red hair with a mind of its own. But she has what doctors like to call ADHD. Meredith struggled mightily in classrooms. She blurted out constantly, had a hard time staying in her seat, and focusing for more than two minutes at a time was a huge challenge for YEARS.

Some teachers were not interested in working with Meredith or our family to help her adjust to school. Others were angels who changed her life. Those amazing teachers helped Meredith find her true self. That's why she became a science teacher; so that she could be a loving adult presence for kids who don't fit into the traditional mold.

I gave her the first copy of the book the day she graduated from college.

I asked Anderson about how readers have been affected by Zoe. "Interestingly enough, I've heard from both parents of ADHD kids *and* parents of kids with brilliant red hair! Both appreciated the chance that the story gave them to let their kids be comfortable in their own skins and celebrate all that they have to give to the world."[1]

In the classroom, introducing stories that include special needs individuals as the protagonist or secondary character promotes awareness and understanding. Stories that share well-developed characters, universal themes, evocative settings, problems, crises, and resolutions are a step toward imagining the lives of others. Such stories differentiate from exploiting pitiful limitations by exploring healthy differences and illuminating the spirit of possibilities. Promoting characters with diverse intelligences and physical abilities pushes readers to step beyond their insular perceptions of themselves and a skewed sense of *normal.*

Rick Riordan spoke about Percy Jackson, the half-blood protagonist in *The Lightning Thief* (the first title in the wildly popular Percy Jackson and the Olympians series), "I originally invented Percy as a character for stories that I told my son at bedtime . . . My son has ADHD just like Percy. I feel that ADHD kids are the divergent thinkers. Later in life, they are the most successful adults. They're the ones who are in demand by companies that want employees who think 'outside the box.'"[2]

Riordan's understanding and compassion for children with learning disabilities contribute immensely to the credibility of his characters. Riordan explains, "I've always been into Greek mythology. Greek myths are all about the hero. The hero has a destiny and must overcome great odds. Myths explain things that are otherwise unexplainable."[3] Riordan creates characters like Percy—stressed-out failures in the classroom—capable of dealing with larger-than-life challenges. Percy is assertive and impulsive. He faces his disabilities, the pangs of teen angst, and his family's dysfunctions. He acts now and thinks later; he disrupts the status quo to battle evil, avenge the meek, and save the world. No small feat for a kid who's been butted out of almost every school he's attended. Thus Percy, underdog turned hero, attracts teen fellowship (and readership) with a fast devotion. Riordan says that his favorite feedback to his Percy Jackson titles comes from reluctant and dyslexic readers "who tell me *The Lightning Thief* was the first book they ever read on their own. That is the best encouragement I could ever get to keep writing."[4]

In Katherine Hannigan's story *True (. . . Sort Of)* we follow main character, Delly, who is filled with exuberance and a bubbly good nature—until fifth grade. At that point her energy gets in the way of classroom management, and Delly's good humor becomes hackled with trouble. Her spirit dwindles, her attitude plunges, and she becomes more problem than positive contributor. While Delly's situation is an aside to the story of her classmate who protects a scary secret, it is the very nature of Delly's impetuous personality that is the catalyst that drives the overarching tale. The reader discovers that without Dilly's uninhibited curiosity, brash behavior, and bold personality, her friend's secret will stay a festering abuse under an impenetrable veil of feigned parental care.

A language arts teacher recently had her students reading Jerry Spinelli's *Loser*. She said, "*Loser* should be required reading in fourth grade." The novel is about simple Donald Zinkoff, who wholeheartedly and joyfully embraces his elementary school experience. When the other children recognize that Donald's exuberant spirit does not conform to their acceptable group behavior, he is teased for his silliness. When his clumsy excitement contributes to the loss of the class's annual relay race, he is taunted, jeered, and ostracized. Consequently, the innocence of childhood evaporates from the elementary school culture. The teacher explained that many of her students responded with empathy toward Donald, but others said, "Well, he was asking for it!" This is exactly the conversation we want to have with students, to figure out why they treat others in a certain way. Why is it okay? Why does the A grade make you feel good and anything lower makes you feel less? Where does the quest for one-upmanship come from? Why do we critically judge ourselves? When does personal acceptance disappear? Such questions may never be resolved. Reading *Loser* can prompt classroom conversations and encourage students to consider the differences within themselves and register the differences all around them. It's a step toward empathy and understanding.

When Chris Crutcher speaks about his volatile autistic character Telephone Man, he does so with humor. A dose of humor is necessary armor against the brewing anger unleashed from some learning disabled children. Telephone Man is a fictionalized character based on a student Crutcher knew when he was the head of a K–12 last-chance alternative school. "Telephone Man is autistic, but about telephones, he's a savant. He followed the telephone repairman all around our school, looking over his shoulder, correcting him and arguing about what wires went where. The repairman hated him because Telephone Man drove him crazy and because Telephone Man was always right. . . . When [Telephone Man] was angry, he would fly into my office arriving feet first, swearing angrily. If the door was closed, he would kick it open, blowing it off its hinges. We learned not to latch the door."[5] There are few teachers who have not had a Telephone Man to deal with. Instead of letting them unhinge you, unhinge the doors that lock them out.

Jack Gantos is the author of the Joey Pigza books, about a bighearted kid with a dysfunctional family and a zany, over-the-top ADHD high-wired brain. Joey thinks the same strange thoughts as other kids, but he neglects to consider the consequences. He has a thought and he acts on it. He swallows his house key that's attached to a string, pulling it back up over and over again to amuse his classmate until he swallows it, completely forgetting it no longer has the string attached. He sticks his finger in the pencil sharpener. Joey's antics grab the reader's attention and are the real-life stuff that turns a classroom into mayhem. School psychologists recommend that elementary school faculty read *Joey Pigza Swallowed the Key.* Gantos has said about his stories, "Comedy is used deliberately; it shifts tense family dynamics and relaxes an emotional and sometimes physical crisis. I use it as a bait to draw readers in; it's a trap. In the Joey books there's a lot of action up top riding the surface, and a lot of tension below; a hammer-and-anvil technique. Humor is the magician's way to distract your eye while the trick is being played."[6] Humor hooks many young readers, encouraging them to keep reading. The tension leads them to awareness, and in some cases, personal reflection.

Eleven years after the publication of *Joey Pigza Swallowed the Key*, I asked Gantos about reader response to the books. He wrote,

> When I write a book I have a general sense of the audience I'm writing for, but largely I'm more concerned with the construction of the book: the characters, story line, measure of humor and pathos, the language and so forth. The writing of the book is what I can control, and when the book is finished and launched and passed into the hands of readers, I then lose control of the material because the book is never read by anyone as I read it. Each reader has a distinct interpretation of the text, and my window into that interpretation is through the letters readers send me.
>
> With the Joey Pigza books I have received thousands of letters from readers, and the letters share two distinct reader responses. The first is: "How did you know I feel this way inside?" And the second is: "I know a kid like Joey in my class and he's driving us nuts, but now that I know how he feels inside I'll give him a second chance."
>
> These two responses hit the nail on the head. When I read a book I am after the exact same results: through the text I want to know myself better, and I want to gain an expanded insight into others. The readers of the Joey Pigza books are no different. In their letters they tell me that through Joey's

descriptions of his feelings that they now have the words to define their own attention deficit issues, and family and friend conflicts. They find a way to articulate who they are to themselves, and to others. And by my good fortune, they sit down and write me. If I had to guess, I would say the most popular phrase in all the letters is, "How did you know . . ." When a child reads a book and by surprise finds themselves in it, it is a powerful moment of self-discovery and definition. And when reading a book allows a young reader to see more deeply into others, it is the caring gift of empathy that they are compelled to practice.

I have penned the books, but it is clear to me that it is the readers who have paged into their own lives and the lives of others to better know who they are and how we are all related through a common humanity. When I read the stacks of letters I receive from Joey Pigza readers it is as if I am discovering the hidden files of Joey's life—it is always the readers who are putting literature into action and breathing life into the lungs of the book.[7]

Suggested Reading

Juby, Susan

Alice, I Think

Perfection Learning Prebound, 2004   Grades 8–12

emotional issues, social issues

Alice's transition from homeschooling to high school is not going well. Without friends and now in search of the perfect look and hairstyle, she comes across as a bit different. Her offbeat if well-intentioned mother isn't much help. Nonetheless, Alice is a keen observer, and her unusual perspective is hilarious. She's a smart teen bemused by the oddities of life, perplexed by social situations, and irritated with her less-than-effective psychologist.

Crutcher, Chris

Athletic Shorts: Six Short Stories

Greenwillow Books, 1991   Grades 8–12

AIDS, Asperger's syndrome, autism, homophobia, homosexuality, learning disability, physical disability

This is a hard-hitting collection of short stories revisiting many characters from Crutcher's previous novels, all emotionally charged and pitted against family or social issues. Of particular interest for this section is "Telephone Man." The story's narrator and conflicted protagonist, Telephone Man is a teen whose behaviors and internal mulling clearly land him on the autism spectrum. For him, perhaps a larger challenge than autism is understanding the mixed messages from his racist father, a man who uses the "N word" at home but acts respectfully to the face of a black man. Telephone Man's limited and rigid knowledge, reinforced and influenced by his father's embittered racism, is thoroughly confused by his father's two-faced behavior. When a black boy rescues him from a gang of Asian bullies, Telephone Man's perspective is rattled, his confusion intense, and his own racist attitude challenged in the face of reality.

Teen boys who have Asperger's syndrome will totally get this short glimpse of Telephone Man's achievements and conflicts: his hypersensitive reaction to touch, noise, light; how he clings to right and wrong, black and white; and his passionate focus— working with telephones. He is confused by inference; for example, shampoos that have labels with pictures of strawberries and that smell like strawberries but, when slugged down, are sickening, perplex and stun. Telephone Man is slowly awakening to the reality that everything is *not* black or white—including people. It may be the most difficult work that someone with Asperger's (or anyone else) will contend with.

Peirce, Lincoln

Big Nate: In a Class by Himself

Harper, 2010   Grades 4–6

behavioral issues, social issues

Sixth-grader Nate has a problem with organization and behavior. Everything is going wrong—and his multiple detentions aren't helping. When a fortune cookie foretells that his bad luck is about to change, look out! Fans of the Wimpy Kid and Origami Yoda series will love the clever graphic comic novels of Big Nate.

Bauer, Joan

Close to Famous

Viking Juvenile, 2011   Grades 6–8

learning disability, reading disability

Foster McFee is dragging her feet toward seventh grade in a new school, in a new town. Daddy died in the Iraq war, and Foster misses him every day of her life. She and Mama have fled from Mama's abusive ex-boyfriend—an Elvis impersonator—and landed in Culpepper, Virginia, a sleepy little town filled with feisty and winsome characters.

Additional Titles of Interest Featured in Other Chapters

Boys of Steel: The Creators of Superman (chapter 6, page 91)

Helen Keller: Rebellious Spirit (chapter 5, page 68)

Radiance Descending (chapter 7, page 111)

Here is a place where kind folks invite Foster and Mama to live in their old customized Airstream RV that rests in the backyard.

In the midst of this unusual new start, Foster focuses her positive energy on what she does best: baking. She's become a pro at baking muffins and cupcakes; when she delivers her baked goods to the local diner, those folks can't get enough of them.

Meanwhile, Foster hates thinking about seventh grade and the heap of frustration and shame that will no doubt go along with it. In an unlikely twist of fate, she falls into favor with a local movie star, a celebrity who is hiding from personal tough times and heartache. Foster wheedles her way into Ms. Charleena's good life and good graces—and vice versa. Ms. Charleena lifts herself out of her self-imposed melancholy and takes a hard look at what's happening in her very own kitchen: a child who can't read hides under Foster's brave façade. Shaking off her own drama, Charleena takes on the charge of teaching a kid to read. This story is not so much about Foster's reading disability as it is about capitalizing on and celebrating your strengths. Foster doesn't let her losses consume her and makes the most of her wins. She overlooks her troubles and places her energy into her love of baking. Along with her cupcakes comes a tremendous amount of goodwill. Foster pushes through hard times and strives to rise above the tough stuff.

~~~~~~

Sachar, Louis
Dogs Don't Tell Jokes
Knopf, 1991   Grades 4–8
behavioral issues, nonconformity, social issues

Seventh-grader Gary is determined to be a stand-up comic—from home to school. Unfortunately, he has an unappreciative audience, and everyone is more annoyed with Gary than amused. Gary seems clueless and absorbs the impatient stings over and over again from all who suffer him. He is blessed with an ever-present optimism that won't be squelched by naysayers. Gary is a character whom readers will learn from and be inspired by. His beguiling personality is the winning combination against the negative feedback he receives. He is true to himself. He opens up a worldview past socially imposed limitations and shortsighted rejection of creative differences.

Giff, Patricia Reilly

Eleven

Wendy Lamb Books, 2008   Grades 4–6
dyslexia, reading disability

Sam is haunted by letters—they create a cryptic puzzle that he can't solve because he can't read. He is also haunted by the symbolism of the number 11. Just two straight lines, he reasons; could be a number on a street address, two straight trees against the sky or maybe two towering spires of a castle? Searching the attic for hidden birthday presents one day, Sam uncovers a secret that intensifies his irrational fear: a newspaper clipping reveals his 3-year-old face. Sam sounds out one word, "missing," but he can't read the other clues . . .

Sam is smart, creative, and cagey. He has learned to compensate for his dyslexia and strikes up a friendship with a new girl at school—a "reader." What begins from necessity and convenience evolves into a genuine friendship of support, respect, and acceptance. But with his newfound friendship comes questions toward the mysterious magazine clipping, his loving grandpa, and their devoted, culturally mixed family of friends. The unraveling of Sam's past will intrigue readers.

Philbrick, Rodman

Freak the Mighty

Blue Sky Press, 1993   Grades 6–9
death, family trauma, learning disability, physical disability

Max's learning disabled classes make little difference; he's still unable to read or write. He is looking at a lousy summer between a miserable seventh-grade experience and the looming doom of the upcoming eighth grade. He calls himself "butthead" or "goon," the result of the all-too-believable taunting and teasing from peers. His self-image is shattered, and a traumatic past is a secret he fears to remember. Then Kevin moves in next door. They knew each other in day care, when Max was known as Kicker—he kicked out at anybody who dared touch him. Kevin called himself Robot Man—he was little, with crooked legs that had metal braces running alongside them. Now Max is scary big—much bigger than the rest—and Kevin, with leg braces and crutches, is too small. Kevin is also whip-smart and imaginative. These two unusual boys become an unlikely team, calling themselves Freak the Mighty. Max hoists Kevin on his shoulders, and like medieval knights they set off on great adventures, to slay the dragons of their town, outwit the local thugs, entangle with evil, mayhem, murder, and escape. This is a weird yet fabulous story celebrating oddities, quirks and the power of friendship. Alas, Kevin's good heart is too big for his little body, and harsh reality catches up. Kids will see beyond two freaky boys with the cards stacked against them, and know instead two friends who pull off one heroic deed after another while they pull for each other. *Freak the Mighty* is about overcoming adversity, but more accurately, it's an action-packed adventure that grabs life's challenges head on and pits them against the faith, encouragement, and fortitude of strong friendships. Original and refreshing.

Keyes, Daniel

Flowers for Algernon

Harcourt, Brace and World, 1966   Grade 9–adult
mental disability
Note: Includes disturbing emotional content, bullying, abuse, and mature sexual situations

This 1959 classic novella later became the full-length book (and movie) *Flowers for Algernon*, about mentally challenged 32-year-old Charlie. Charlie is a kindhearted, simple man who enjoys his cleaning job at a bakery and the friends that he has there. With an IQ of 68, he is eager to work; he wants to be helpful and wants to learn to read, write, and improve his memory. It is when he observes Algernon, a lab mouse who is given experimental brain surgery—and becomes super smart—that Charlie's simple world begins to shift. He enthusiastically volunteers to be the first human to undergo experimental brain surgery. And for a time, he experiences a taste of high intellect and develops a romantic relationship. Bit by bit, with the assistance of a beautiful and compassionate teacher, he has fulfilling and emotional experiences. Smart Charlie understands that his bakery coworkers were never laughing *with* him. Now they resent his accomplishments and hate him for his achievements. With his newly acquired intelligence, Charlie reflects upon his past and current relationships; the revelations are disturbing and sad. As his intelligence exceeds the genius level, Charlie is poignantly aware that he is alone, and that his gains are not what he expected or everlasting.

Charlie's transitions are jarring, but his transformation occurs when he accepts that it's not merely intelligence or psychology but also human relationships that sustain us. Within this novel are considerations of huge proportions: conflicts in scientific progress; the irony of getting what you wish for; the complexities of emotional awareness; bullying; and insincere, opportunistic, and tenuous human relationships. Although *Flowers for Algernon* does contend with difficult subject matter, it is a meaningful book to process within a reading group.

Anderson, Laurie Halse, and Ard Hoyt
The Hair of Zoe Fleefenbacher Goes to School
Simon and Schuster Books for Young Readers, 2009   Grades K–2
ADHD, compulsive behavior, impulsiveness

In this picture book we join Zoe and her long, red, radiantly rampant hair. Zoe's zesty, zealous locks are having a ball and stirring up a sensation. To follow Zoe and her unwieldy hair is to rush along on a free-spirited jaunt. The tendrils wave, they squiggle, and they dash to perform multiple tasks: they like turning on the TV, pouring a glass of juice, petting the cat—all at once. They brush Zoe's teeth, pick out her clothes, and pack her lunch before she's out the door. Her parents think her hair is beautiful; it is the marvel of her kindergarten class. Then first grade strikes, and things change. Zoe's new teacher is not so enamored by her fabulous hair. A serious undertaking to control the wisps of tangential interests, the nonconforming tendrils, the exuberant energy, is about to begin. How Zoe learns to control and focus energy toward group tasks, without losing her creative bounce, is a celebration of positive teacher/student interaction and natural development.

Lubar, David
Hidden Talents / True Talents
Tom Doherty Associates, 1999 / Starscape, 2007   Grades 7–9
behavioral issues, emotional issues, learning disability

In *Hidden Talents*, 13-year-old Martin and his gang of misfits have been called losers for so long that they now believe it. Boarding in an alternative school for rejects and problem students, the boys unwittingly exhibit destructive psychic powers that get them into deeper trouble. Martin recognizes the boys' psychic talents, helps them to develop and control their psychic potential, and in doing so, finally discovers something good about himself. (*Hidden Talents* is the first book of several in a series).

True Talents marks the return of the paranormal pack of misfits. The boys have escaped the confines of their alternative school and are on the loose in this action-packed adventure. They attempt to control their secret powers, though not always in the most appropriate ways (like when one of the boys tests his telekinesis in a bank by teleporting cash to his pocket). Individually, they have each dealt with misunderstanding, mistrust, and rejection. With their friendships they've discovered inner strength and renewed self-esteem. These witty boys get themselves into deep trouble and emerge heroic, discovering that with power comes responsibility. Author Lubar's hidden power is embedding sly humor into an interesting literary format that includes easy-to-read e-mails, letters, newspaper columns, and journal entries.

Sitomer, Alan Lawrence

Homeboyz

Jump at the Sun / Hyperion Books for Children, 2007   Grades 8–12
behavioral issues, death, emotional issues, learning disability, trauma

Teddy's younger sister is the fatal victim of a drive-by shooting. Computer hacking and vigilante vengeance are Teddy's tools to avenge her. When the tables turn and Teddy ends up in jail, his parole officer has some creative rehab strategies. Tutoring an underprivileged at-risk kid isn't Teddy's idea of progress, but in the end, it makes a difference in the vicious cycle of inner-city war games. This is an action-packed novel that teens love.

Gantos, Jack

Joey Pigza Swallowed the Key

Farrar, Straus and Giroux, 1998   Grades 4–6
ADHD, compulsive behavior, social issues

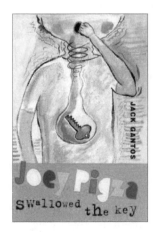

Traveling in Joey's high-wired body is a good way to learn what ADHD feels like. Stuck in overdrive and often out of control, Joey plunges through life like the Tasmanian devil. He's compulsive, impulsive, and driven by good intentions gone bad. What looks funny and crazy on the outside has a much different perspective through Joey's lens. Flawed family dynamics exacerbate his condition. From the chain-smoking grandma to the lame-duck estranged father, a jumbled gene pool seems to undermine his mother's attempt at intervention. If there were ever a book to help develop compassion toward those wild ADHD kids, this is it.

Riordan, Rick

The Lightning Thief

Percy Jackson and the Olympians series, Book 1.
Miramax Books / Hyperion Books for Children, 2005   Grades 4–8
dyslexia, learning disability

Who knew that a story about a dyslexic teen hanging with a bunch of campy Greek gods and goddesses would turn into a blockbuster series? Twelve-year-old Percy Jackson is stewing in frustration over his ADHD learning disabilities. As crazy luck would have it, Percy lands in a boot camp for half-bloods who are training to hone their mythological battle skills. Here they are governed by idiosyncratic Greek gods and goddesses, and an action-packed adventure unfolds. Percy has conflicted feelings when he learns that he too is a half-blood—his dad the mighty Poseidon and his mom a mighty-loving mortal. But he takes it all in stride. He's sent on daring quests, and he discovers he has phenomenal (and sometimes problematic) powers. Percy straddles his two worlds with self-deprecating humor and incredulous gumption. He is an inspiring hero for underachievers and lovers of a great story.

Spinelli, Jerry

Loser

Paw Prints, 2008   Grades 4–7
bullying, nonconformity, social issues

When Donald Zinkoff runs off with gusto to grab his first taste of first grade, he is one exuberant, wildly enthusiastic kid. He hugs life tight and squeezes out all things fabulous. He is unabashedly unaware of his overzealous ways and is clueless about appearances. His classmates laugh with him, at first, but as they grow past their own innocence, they slowly absorb the cautious inhibitions of growing up. By fifth grade, they're laughing at him. At the end of the school year's field day, it's earnest and well-intentioned Donald Zinkoff who bungles the class race. His teammates target their fury at him, calling him loser. He absorbs their cruel behavior into himself, reeling his way home. This is growing up? School, that place he loved, now carries shame. He skips a day. Inadvertently he spends it with an elderly lady who is ever so slow. She creeps along with her walker, bringing peanut butter sandwiches to the table. She is kind, in no rush, and listens. Zinkoff recognizes a kinder side of life. His guileless happiness is renewed. His classmates' rancor is softened. He navigates outside the pack and resumes his gleeful nature. When a little girl goes missing on a cold and snowy night, we see the winning core of Donald Zinkoff, who risks his own safety. Zinkoff's unwavering conscience is the stuff of heroes.

Gibson, William

The Miracle Worker

Bantam Books, 1975   Grade 7–12
blindness, deafness, emotional issues, visual impairment

This 1957 3-act play by William Gibson is based on Helen Keller's autobiography, *The Story of My Life*. Though written in play format, it is an easy and compelling story to follow. A young blind, deaf, and feral-behaving Helen has been chalked up as a disabled loss by physicians and her family. Her family pities and spoils her to excess. Enter Anne Sullivan, a teacher who is also partially blind and has been trained (and raised) at the famous Perkins Institute for the Blind. Anne is challenged with the seemingly impossible feat of teaching the horribly spoiled Helen. Indeed it is a miracle of faith that her parents release control of their young "helpless" daughter to what they perceive as cruel treatment and misunderstanding from Anne Sullivan. The essence of this story is that Helen's largest handicap is her overly protective family. Anne Sullivan unlocks Helen's prison of isolation by teaching the young girl how to communicate. Helen Keller becomes one of the most incredible and motivational women of the 1950s and 1960s. Her journey from being a helpless, hopeless child whose best chance of life was institutional residence, to being able to communicate with others, be politically active, and change lives through her brilliance and her inspirational story is miraculous. This slight play will make a huge impact on the way students see special needs individuals, and more excitingly, how they see the potential within themselves.

Winkler, Henry, and Lin Oliver

Niagara Falls, or Does It?

Grosset and Dunlap, 2003   Grades 3–5

dyslexia, learning disability

Fourth-grader Hank has trouble with reading and writing. For Hank the dictionary is a "useless," frustrating tool. He bemoans, "I can't spell words because I can't sound them out. So how am I going to find them in the dictionary if I can't spell them in the first place?" (p. 22). Hank may have trouble in school, but he has a good point. Fortunately for us, Hank has the gift of making kids laugh. His fourth-grade teacher, Ms. Adolf, admonishes, "Fourth-graders laugh way too much." But when Ms. Adolf assigns the class a five-paragraph summer vacation essay, Hank is not laughing. Adding to the pressure, Ms. Adolf targets Hank as the first student to read his essay out loud in class. And so begins his all-out venture to avoid the written assignment and instead design an amazing display, a presentation that will blow Ms. Adolf out of the water with its ingenuity. Hank and his friends mastermind a Niagara Falls display, but the rigged-up cardboard plumbing is faulty. The day of the presentation, water spills into the classroom and Hank's plans to impress Ms. Adolf take an ugly turn. Punished with in-school detention and grounded to his bedroom to write the dreaded essay, the 9-year-old energetic and once-happy kid muses, "I hated my room. I hated my assignment. I hated my brain. Why couldn't I write or spell or add or divide? Forget about multiplying . . . It's like my mind is a chalkboard and the words just slide off it in the time it takes to walk [to school]" (p. 55). This is a clever, funny, and insightful story about a boy's best intentions being derailed by his learning disabilities. With gusto and grit Hank contends with his chronic battle against classroom doom with the help of another teacher. This bright, funny, well-meaning boy's failures are plausible, but his rescue comes just in time.

Schmidt, Gary D.

Okay for Now

Clarion Books, 2011   Grades 8–12

dyslexia, family issues

Eighth-grader Doug, the youngest of three brothers, has just moved to an upstate New York mill town. He's the new kid in town and not at all thrilled with how the town—or life in their "dump" of a house—is turning out. When young Lil, daughter of the local deli owner, befriends Doug, his life takes incremental shifts. First she introduces him to the library, a place that shouldn't have much appeal for a boy with a reading disability, except it does. The library holds an original copy of John James Audubon's *Birds of America*. Doug, supported by the caring attention of an aging librarian, is transformed. He is transformed from a tough guy whose major passion is baseball to being open to other pursuits, aesthetic, cultural, intellectual, and emotional. When Doug's older brother returns from Vietnam, psychologically and physically wounded, the story takes a pivotal turn. The despair and negative future that the "dump" symbolizes is eroded by the kindness of others. The rare and tenuous beauty of Audubon's birds flutter metaphorically as an introductory foreshadow to each chapter. A story that carries strife, conflict, and discord lurks in the corners of every page, but beauty and redemption win out. Doug is a witty, delightful, and refreshing character made all the more so by navigating his way through the ugliness and keeping his heart open to possibilities.

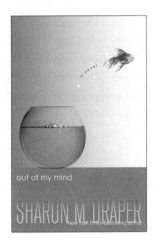

Draper, Sharon M.

Out of My Mind

Atheneum Books for Young Readers, 2010   Grades 5–8
cerebral palsy

Born with cerebral palsy, Melody is almost 11 years old and has never spoken a word. Feeling the sting of an adolescent girl trying to make friends in a fifth-grade class is rough, but Melody's world is tragically complicated. She's mostly placed in the special ed classroom, where education means being babysat in a room with cartoon reruns and nursery tunes. She is a brilliant fifth grader trapped in an uncontrollable body. Her world is enhanced by insight and intellect and shortchanged by physical limitations and misunderstandings. She'll never sing or dance, talk on the phone, or whisper secrets to her friends.

Melody's not complaining; she's planning and fighting the odds. In her court are supportive family members, good neighbors, and an attentive student teacher. Pitted against her is the "normal" world: schools with limited resources, cliquish girls, superficial assumptions, and the stigma of disability. Kids and adults will benefit from meeting Melody and her gutsy, candid, compelling story. It speaks volumes and reveals the quiet strength and fortitude it takes to overcome disabilities and the misconceptions that go with them.

Lord, Cynthia
Rules

Scholastic Press, 2006   Grades 4–8

autism, cerebral palsy, mutism, paralysis

Twelve-year-old Catherine can't wait for summer and making new friends. She's also dreading looking after her autistic little brother, David, with his many embarrassing behaviors. The title refers to David's black-and-white world, a world of rules: no toys in the fish bowl, chew with your mouth closed, and keep your pants on. Catherine knows that the world is not that simple and explains to David, "Sometimes people laugh when they like you. But sometimes they laugh to hurt you" (p. 90). Resignedly, Catherine spends much of her summer helping to care for her brother; at the therapy clinic, Catherine meets and befriends Jason, a nonverbal paraplegic who uses a book of pictures to communicate. With Jason's friendship, Catherine meets head-on her own doubts and discriminations toward people with special needs. She faces what it truly means to be friends. This is not only Catherine's, David's, or their parents' story but also a story about the dynamics of living with a disability, accepting one another's flaws and foibles, and seeing the value of family.

Byars, Betsy Cromer, and Constantinos Coconis
The Summer of the Swans

Viking Press, 1970   Grades 4–6

mental disability, self-esteem

Fourteen-year-old Sara wears bright orange sneakers; she wishes she were pretty and popular and had a normal little brother. Her mother died when she was 8, and she and her siblings live with their aunt. She misses her absent father, who works far away and visits only on some weekends. Though she fiercely loves her mentally disabled younger brother, Charlie, she is obsessed with her own problems, not his. When Charlie leaves the house one night and becomes lost, Sara learns what it means to care about someone more than yourself. This is a nonpreachy story that is as suspenseful as it is heartwarming. The story's themes are as poignantly effective today as when the book received the Newbery Medal in 1971.

Anderson, Laurie Halse

Teacher's Pet #7

Vet Volunteer series. Puffin Books, 2009   Grades 4–7

blindness, learning disability

Maggie enters her seventh-grade biology classroom burdened by everything that spoils her daily life: school. When she sees Scout, a beautiful German shepherd lying at Mr. Carlson's feet, all dread drops away, and she thinks this class might be different. Her teacher, Mr. Carlson, is recently blind, and his dog, Scout, is his working companion. This class *is* different, but some things remain the same: Maggie is frustrated by reading trouble, elusive study skills, and her inability to retain what is said in class. Yet her experience with, intuition of, and ability to handle animals is keen.

Mr. Carlson considers Scout a tool; he's not so great with dogs but is pretty good with teens. He and Maggie make a pact: Mr. Carlson will work at giving Scout positive attention, and she'll work on staying focused in class and doing her homework. The Timmy/Lassie wholesomeness of this story is upped with Maggie, a likeable imperfect protagonist with more than a touch of sass.

Sachar, Louis

There's a Boy in the Girls' Bathroom

Knopf, 1987   Grades 4–7

behavioral issues, learning disability

Bradley, the oldest boy in his fifth-grade class, is friendless. And no wonder: he lies, he's sarcastic, and he's a bully. His schoolwork and homework are a mess. At home he plays with his damaged toy animals, revealing his insecurities and vulnerabilities, and you can't help but pull for him. Through routine visits with a compassionate and good-humored school counselor, Bradley learns to like himself and accept others. His poignant need for acceptance coupled with his self-protective, biting barbs of verbal abuse is painfully real. Readers may see bits of themselves hidden under the many layers of Bradley's armor.

Hannigan, Katherine

True (. . . Sort Of)

Greenwillow Books, 2011   Grades 5–7

abuse, family life/conflict, friendship, selective mutism

Delly's life is patchy with the ups and downs of being a feisty redhead with a raspy voice and a thirst for excitement, generally acting as the thorn in the side of a big broody family. She is bubbly, happy, and near bursting with energy. It is this very same zest for life that ends up getting her in trouble around fifth grade, when her verve is considered disruptive, her enthusiasm a classroom nuisance. Then Ferris Boyd comes to town, a girl so slight, hunched, and drawn into herself that she's mistaken for a boy. Before she arrives, the teacher forewarns the class, "She can hear, but does not speak. In addition, she must not be touched" (p. 61). Delly's insatiable curiosity kicks in, and she becomes intrigued with the peculiar Ferris. She stalks and follows her home, discovering Ferris's father's big green car parked in the driveway—a foreboding symbol. Fortunately it's rarely there. With Delly's persistence, soon the two girls become fast friends. Like an animal, Ferris Boyd speaks with the soulfulness of her eyes. When that is not enough, she occasionally writes notes. They spend after-school hours hidden in the sanctuary of a tree house and the serenity of the surrounding woods.

Ferris is loaded with mystery. Another side of her life is her passion and skill with basketball; she spends hours playing alone on a remote court. Once again, she is spied upon—this time by a boy, impassioned by the game and mesmerized by her ability. She befriends this lone young basketball player who is riddled with a stutter and low confidence. Soon she is helping him overcome his internal obstacles and focus on the game.

Not too much happens in this little novel. Oftentimes it seems like an idyllic adventure of kids cocooned in their protective woodlands or spending carefree hours on the basketball court. It is the undercurrent of Ferris Boyd's timid ways and Delly's determination to pierce the silent fear that captures the reader's interest. That Ferris Boyd is being abused by her father is not much of a shock. The steadfast support of friendship and Ferris's ultimate courage is the success of this story.

Galante, Cecilia
Willowood
Aladdin, 2010   Grades 5–8
Down syndrome, family trauma

When Lily lands a job at the local pet store, things in her new city neighborhood begin to look up. The store's owner entrusts her to care for hatching the iguana eggs that would otherwise be disposed of. Not only does Lily take on that cause, but she begins a tenuous friendship with the owner's son, Nate, an adult with Down syndrome. Nate's behavior is frequently erratic, overly sensitive, and emotional. He lost his mother when he was too young to understand and hasn't budged past that trauma. Lily discovers that Nate, who is different as well as difficult, is also needy and caring. She learns to think things through from Nate's perspective, engaging in life in a challenging, fragile, and meaningful way that she previously avoided.

NOTES

1. Laurie Halse Anderson explains her family's experience with ADHD.
2. Alison Follos, "Author Profile: Rick Riordan," *Library Media Connection* 26, no. 5 (February 2008): 44.
3. Ibid.
4. Rick Riordan, e-mail to the author, July 2, 2007.
5. Alison Follos, "Author Profile: The 3 C's of Chris Crutcher," *Library Media Connection* 25, no. 3 (November/December 2006): 43.
6. Alison Follos, "Gantos Is Seriously Funny," *Library Media Connection* 23, no. 4 (January 2005): 51.
7. Jack Gantos, letter to the author, September 12, 2011.

four

Stories That Tell Secrets

Emotional and Psychological Issues including Anorexia,
Self-Medicating, Alcoholism, Cutting, Suicide, and Abuse

Books that deal with difficult and dark subject matter that nobody wants to talk about—this is what teens are talking about! Teens are masters of melodrama, and it's likely that traditionally notable titles will circulate freely; *Go Ask Alice* and *The Bell Jar* come to mind. Titles that students recommend to other students are titles to learn about. Perhaps as important, they are titles to share with other teachers and parents—because students already know about them. Books that tackle depression, anorexia, bulimia, cutting, substance abuse, and suicide may not be tops on your booktalk list, but don't ignore them. If you're a librarian, call these titles to your school counselor's attention, ask for time to mention some new titles during faculty meetings, suggest that the English class use one in a literary circle, or select one for a teen book club and invite a counselor to join the discussion. If you're a parent, share these stories with other parents and suggest reading one in your book club.

If teens don't find stories of conflict and discomfort available in the library, they will find them elsewhere. There's a glut of negative, exploitive, sensationalized tabloid news stories bent on shock and reaction. Those aren't the stories we're talking about here.

Not having well-crafted and intentionally selected literature that deals with difficult subject matter in your collection won't protect students from themselves—it will only protect you from uncomfortable interaction or confrontation. The books and stories aren't the danger. Not admitting there's a problem, not having discussions about story content, not processing the conflict inherent in, the situation, *not talking to teens*—that's the danger. Many stories can take readers along into a living hell, but the best ones (for my money) take you there and then offer reflection and resolution. No miracles, but a realistic message of hard work, fortitude from adversity, not bailing out, the grounding knowledge that you're not alone, strength to go through the dark and come out the other side. As author Chris Crutcher says, "If you have trauma in life, that's forever. There's no magic to wipe it away. But if a person shares their story with another person, they become stronger. They have twice as much power to survive."[1]

Self-Harm

There are many stories that teens are fascinated with; this includes books on self-harm, whether the specific subject is substance abuse, cutting, eating disorders, or any number of destructive trends. If you want a sure-thing book for a glowering teen reader, choose a dark, depressing, sex-and-drugs-at-the-precipice-of-death–type story. Girls have an insatiable curiosity about teen behaviors. Even the most well-adjusted young girls— outwardly comfortable, socially and academically successful—have appetites for the dark stuff. Boys also flock toward such books, though they might play it cool and downplay their interest. *Go Ask Alice,* a teen drug abuser's journal published forty years ago, continues to be a hit. More recently, Ned Vizzini's *It's Kind of a Funny Story* circulates through male readers with a life of its own. I suspected the attraction was sex, swearing, and drugs. Not completely so. It has solid substance and is about an overachieving teen's internal battle against his self-inflicted fierce academic pressure, his breakdown, and his slow and oftentimes humorous recovery in a psychiatric ward. There are edgy moments, fast girls, and freaky patients, but nothing untoward. The young author has a convincing and credible voice, and his character's suicidal depression is tempered by his connection to others, his personal reflection, his wry humor, and his successful recovery.

There's nothing wrong with being attracted to and fascinated by depressing stories; young readers, like anyone, are generally curious. In some cases, teens *are* participating in self-harm behaviors and destructive patterns. They need to know that they're not alone. The nondescript, steady-turtle teen may act insidiously, hiding his self-harming behavior under a shell of stability. Other young readers may have dispassionate personas and pretend their disability doesn't affect their daily lives. There's also the indifferent "normal" teen who acts immune and ignores the needs of those around her. For all their different personalities, needs, and interests, teens need information. While they aren't overtly asking for help, they are identifying at some level with vulnerable characters.

Sometimes these candid and personal novels become a confessional, a place for the reader to be absolved from the loneliness of their risky secrets. Laurie Halse Anderson says, "A story's secret is only dangerous if it's not told, because then it's not shared, and that's when isolation settles in, followed by depression, giving up, despair and the pointlessness of survival . . . perhaps it's the bare ugly truth that helps teens through the shaming silence. Truth heals and secrets hurt."[2]

Reading about the secret offers an outlet of identity and possible resolution. It is horrible to feel that nobody else has had a similar experience, that the depression is inescapable, and there's no chance of recovery. There is fear that well-crafted disturbing stories encourage a destructively supportive connection between reader and characters. The more likely effect is that the story becomes a mirror that might shed light on the internal battle and support a step toward good health. Reading about it is better than living it.

I asked Laurie Halse Anderson where her groundbreaking novel *Speak* came from. "I woke up with Melinda in my head. She was crying. My daughter was in sixth grade at the time, safely sleeping in her room. It was a pivotal moment of worrying about her and facing what I'd been avoiding. I was raped in ninth grade. I didn't tell anyone about it. Only about 10 percent of my story is in *Speak*." Perhaps Anderson's ability to speak the bare truth helps teens through their own ashamed silence. She continues, "Writing represents my two passions: I really care about teenagers, and I worry that adults don't talk to them enough. Something happens when teens become as tall as we are; something changes about how adults deal with their issues."[3]

In Chris Crutcher's *Chinese Handcuffs* and *Staying Fat for Sarah Byrnes*, characters face psychological abuse, physical disability, and emotional trauma—bad stuff that happens to good kids. Crutcher's victims fight their way through the darkness, often with the support of tuned-in adults and empathetic classmates. The child emerges wounded, not ruined. Asking for help is a tremendous risk for anybody, but for a young person with few life experiences or coping mechanisms, the admission that they need help can be foreign and terrifying. Teens want to be popular, to fit in and appear normal. They don't want to be perceived by their peers as crazy, insane, nuts, unstable, disabled, handicapped, or different. If they don't realize that their fears and conflicting feelings are normal—and combatable—they'll continue to suffer in silence. Crutcher notes, "For the abused child the most powerful control they have is, 'I can keep this a secret.' There are characters in my books that have secrets that they don't want to reveal."[4] His kind of story minimizes the secret of shame and may be the catalyst to seek help.

Anderson underscores this secret-is-power psychology by speaking about her character, Lia in *Wintergirls,* who battles an eating disorder: "For Lia, not eating and keeping the secret makes her strong."[5]

Chris Crutcher writes, "Our schools are filled with kids who have been treated badly all their lives. They don't tell anyone because there is shame in being treated badly.

Many—girls and boys—have been sexually mistreated. Still others struggle in fear with sexual identity. They respond with eating disorders, cutting, suicidal thought or action. I can't tell you how many letters I've received from kids who found a friend in one of my books, a character who speaks to them."[6]

And so, stories that travel down the path of self-harm are important for all. They underscore the point that we are all interconnected. By reading stories that reveal weaknesses, vulnerabilities, and behaviors that take on an energy beyond our control, we gather strength and become aware that we are not alone in our challenges.

Suggested Reading

SELF-HARM

Plath, Sylvia
The Bell Jar

Paw Prints, 2008   Grades 8–12
anxiety, mental illness, suicide

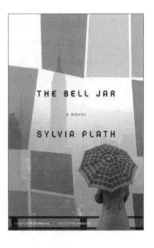

This is the largely autobiographical account of young Esther (Plath), a gifted writer who is excited to begin her summer internship as a junior editor at a New York City magazine in the early 1950s. On the outside Esther has it made: internship, boyfriend, ski vacation in the Adirondacks; but inside she's an overachiever battling a skewed perspective and fraught with anxiety. She's endangered by obsessive suicidal thoughts and, eventually, suicidal attempts. Her descent into insanity is real and harrowing. There's nothing old-fashioned about mental illness, and sixty years after its publication *The Bell Jar* still cuts deep. The absence of melodrama in Esther's voice accentuates the sad, naked fear. One of my students called it "good, but disturbing." Sylvia Plath's understated reality, veiled under a bell jar of depression, is disturbingly convincing.

Walsh, Marissa, ed.
Does This Book Make Me Look Fat?

Clarion Books, 2008   Grades 6–12
eating disorder

A batch of good short stories dealing with bad body images. Many top young adult authors have contributed to the collection, and some of these short stories read better than their novels. Others read like magazine page-turners—making them a sure bet for reluctant readers. Several stories are humorous, some inane, and all are sharp and poignant bites of coping with body image.

Eireann Corrigan's is a particularly frank account of slipping into and coming out the other side of anorexia. She's about to start her new life and is being fitted for her wedding gown. This moment triggers a fear of relapse into an eating disorder that, while far away and long ago, will never completely disappear. She writes,

> My eating disorder had started around my sixteenth birthday. It was like a tornado tore through and afterward nothing looked the same. By the time I recognized myself again, eight years had passed. I spent almost two of those years in treatment facilities. I'd done irreversible damage to my kidneys, developed a heart murmur, and pretty much torpedoed any chance of conceiving children. Anorexia is not like mono—you don't just suddenly catch it. It's not the flu or even the clap. It looked like I'd suddenly gotten obsessed with food, but the truth was I'd never felt comfortable in my body. There was the time I realized that every other girl in fourth grade could turn a cartwheel. And the three months spent sipping Slim-Fast in sixth grade. There was the sweatsuit that I hated—gray with neon triangles all over it. I agonized over wearing that thing, convinced that it made me look fat. A couple weeks ago my mom and I sifted through baby pictures for a wedding day slide show. I found one of the Dreaded Gray Sweatsuit, "How old was I here?" I tapped the picture of the skinny blonde kid with her arms folded across her chest.
>
> And she said, "Six."
>
> So it took me almost a decade to get sick. It's not like I suddenly got better. And usually when I said I was better, I was lying (pp. 24–25).

The confiding honesty in this story is not so much raw as it is comforting. It offers a gentle whisper: *You are not the only one.*

~~~~~~

Sparks, Beatrice

Go Ask Alice

Prentice-Hall, 1971   Grades 8–12
mental illness, suicide

This classic story is wrought with pain and controversy. Forty years after its publication, speculation persists on whether this is the diarist's real entries or a journal tampered with by adults wishing to make a point. Regardless, there is a compelling tone that readers gravitate toward. The anonymous protagonist is under extreme pressure from her "perfect parents" and swings between optimism and despair. She is lonely and needy, an easy victim for a group of fast and superficial friends. When her drink is spiked with LSD, it is the beginning of her uncontrolled journey into darkness. Addiction and irresponsible behaviors follow. As the drugs numb her sensibilities and loneliness, her life drops to suicidal lows.

Vizzini, Ned

It's Kind of a Funny Story

Miramax Books / Hyperion Books
for Children, 2006   Grades 9–12
anxiety, depression, suicide, drug use

Craig is determined to make the grade and score entry into an exclusive "executive pre-professional" high school. He trades friends and fun for a year of unrelenting academic focus. Craig's hard work to get there is his undoing. Attending school with other equally high achievers is like being tossed into a pressure cooker without a release. Surrounded by success-driven classmates, Craig feels alienated, anxious, disillusioned, and depressed. Smoking dope is a lame crutch. He's riddled by insecurity, and his shaky emotional state undermines his intellectual aspirations. Medication helps his depression; yet ironically, once he feels better he decides to stop taking it. One night he stands on the George Washington Bridge, ready to jump. At this emotional precipice, he grasps the last strands of wherewithal and calls a suicide hotline. This single act—Craig reaching out for help—elevates this book above and beyond any other part of the story line. The narrative takes a subtle shift as

Additional Titles of Interest Featured in Other Chapters

Craig's relationships develop and he steps beyond himself. He befriends an eccentric cast of characters and becomes the Jack Nicholson–like hero in a *One Flew Over the Cuckoo's Nest*–type institution (but with a better aftermath!). Craig is genuine, personable, and witty. While the drugs, sexual preoccupation, and dicey language draw teens to the book, it is Craig's courage, candor, recovery, and unique viewpoint that pack the punch. Teens love this book.

Schechter, Lynn R.

My Big Fat Secret: How Jenna Takes Control of Her Emotions and Eating

Magination Press, 2010   Grades 4–6

eating disorder

Jenna is a good-spirited seventh-grade kid with close family ties and good friends. However, adolescence is no walk in the park, and Jenna is bogged down by the extra burden of being overweight. The more she frets and feels depressed about her physical state and the peers who judge her, the more she turns to junk food, a lurking pitfall. Her weight gain makes her feel conspicuous and unattractive. It's a vicious cycle.

The book is highly illustrated, with lots of white space and the approachable and easy-to-read format of e-mail correspondence. Readers follow Jenna's chats with her cousin, her guitar partner and good friend (who happens to be a boy), her parents, and eventually her counselor. In this breezy conversational style Jenna reveals her junk-food demons and confronts her lifestyle. This is a slight story that still manages to dig deep, showing the benefits of gentle support and motivation. It keeps the emotional complexities of the problem from overshadowing the practical and doable strategies.

Anderson, Laurie Halse

Speak

Farrar, Straus and Giroux, 1999   Grades 8–12

date rape, abuse, bullying, mental illness

Speak is Melinda's silently absorbing and sobering secret. When a fun end-of-year high school party turns brutal, Melinda, the panicked victim, calls the cops. In doing so, she becomes a pariah overnight. We follow Melinda through a haunting year. She shuts down, deliberately silencing the inner voice that whispers the unmentionable. She lives in denial, her only outlet being her artwork. She has no friends, no voice, no visible feeling. She's walled herself away from the trauma. This controversial novel, now in its twelfth year of avid readership, gives a scared and socially shunned high school freshman a brave voice to tell the truth and emerge scarred but strong.

Gallo, Donald R., ed.
What Are You Afraid Of?
Stories about Phobias
Candlewick Press, 2006   Grades 6–9
phobia, compulsive behavior

These short stories peer closely at invisible fears that disrupt ordinary life. The selections are by notable authors, some of whom have battled their own phobias and compulsions. Neal Shusterman's eerie "Fear-for-All" is a cautionary tale: Gavin has no compassion for those who are afflicted by phobias. Mysteriously he lands at a special needs school and receives his just desserts when he becomes the school's phobia magnet. He is transmuted into a sin-eater of sorts, absorbing individual phobias and experiencing the terror that plagues each and every member at his school. Alex Flinn's "The Door" tells of a boy whose parents have gone away on vacation and left him in a self-imposed state of house arrest. As his panic increases, the food dwindles. Ron Koertge's "Calle de Muerte" is about a boy who can't cross the street. The beauty of this story is that it's wheelchair-bound Olivia who helps him step, bit by bit, beyond his fear. In Nancy Springer's "Rutabaga," Lydia is the quiet, obliging daughter who won't utter a sharp word against her control-freak perfect mother. She avoids knives because of what they do—or more subtly, what she might do. In Joan Bauer's "Thin," Deenie is compelled to deny her eating disorder as completely as she's obsessed with her exercise routine. In her mind, she rationalizes her behavior as just wanting to be thin, to look good—is that so bad? She loses pounds (and friends) as she works herself into a collapse. No neat and easy solutions among these stories, but the constant affirmation that fear is real and you're not alone. This is an excellent look at hidden fears that are easily dismissed and difficult to understand.

Plum-Ucci, Carol

What Happened to Lani Garver

Harcourt, 2002   Grades 9–12

eating disorder, cancer, homophobia, bullying

Is Lani a hero? Is he an angel? Is he a she? Claire, a cheerleading type, is growing up on "typical" small-town Hackett Island. After a daunting battle with leukemia, she worries that it may be back. Another stalking shadow, if self-perpetuated, is her eating disorder. Enter Lani Garver, tilting at windmills on Claire's behalf, covertly dressing in his mother's clothes and unable to deflect the homophobia that he attracts from the townies. Lani is Claire's emotional savior, and through their friendship she unwittingly draws attention, and cruel hostility toward him. Much to ponder, process, and discuss with teens.

Anderson, Laurie Halse

Wintergirls

Viking, 2009   Grades 8–12

eating disorder, cutting, death

This is an emotional and gritty story of two friends who compete in a deadly contest—who will be skinniest? Cassie "wins"; Lia, wracked by eating issues and self-loathing, is collapsing under the weight of guilt over Cassie's death. Just out of an institution, Lia is under the constant scrutiny of her mother. Yet Lia is stealthy. She returns to her old patterns, careful to hide her cuts to the inside of her thighs, camouflaging her weight loss with clothing, tinkering with the scale—she's incapable of wavering off course from her own demise. Lia's subterfuge is nothing new to a troubled teen. While clearly an unreliable narrator, she's a master of self-deception, misinterpreting her hunger pangs for signs of strength. *Wintergirls*, though fiction, is not make-believe; it offers rich and powerful topics for discussion and could be the beginning of a healthy conversation with any teen with an unhealthy self-perception. Better yet, it may be a conversation that averts a teen descending into that insidious cycle.

SOCIAL DILEMMAS, FAMILY DYSFUNCTION, AND PSYCHOLOGICAL TRAUMA

Plum-Ucci, Carol

The Body of Christopher Creed

Harcourt, 2000 Grades 8–12
death, mental illness

Stumbling over a decomposed body pushes our narrator over the edge. We meet him while he's recovering and retelling the mysterious stream of events that lead up to his breakdown. The mystery pivots around peculiar Christopher, an odd man out who is every bully's target and whom his schoolmates avoid. Hints of family abuse and psychological torment abound. A peculiarly eerie and mysterious tale.

Wynne-Jones, Tim

The Boy in the Burning House

Farrar, Straus and Giroux, 2001 Grades 7–9
psychological abuse, death, recovery

Hypocrisy and self-righteousness flourish within a small town. Two teens work hard to expose the wrongs that townspeople are blind to. Two years after his father's disappearance, Jim still suffers. He befriends odd Ruth Rose as she contends with her own demons (predominantly, a fanatical pastor/stalking stepfather). Meanwhile an unsolved mystery from the past creeps in, setting off a chain of cataclysmic reactions. An entwined knot of suspense by a great storyteller.

Crutcher, Chris

Chinese Handcuffs

Greenwillow Books, 1989 Grades 8–12
physical disability, suicide, sexual abuse

This novel is said to have everything but the kitchen sink in it. Long before Dillon's older brother lost his legs in a motorcycle accident, he teetered on the edge of emotional instability. Now Dillon is tormented with guilt from his past and is dead-set on suicide.

He uses his journal, writing letters to his dead brother, as an attempt to sort out the loss and torment. Dillon becomes involved with a girlfriend who is haunted by the shame of her father's past incestuous advances. Worse, she is now hiding the sexual abuse of her stepfather, a psychopathic predator. Dillon wants to help her, but he's up against an adult who orchestrates a threatening game of diabolical power. This is a psychological thriller. It is also a story of personal trauma, desperation, fear, and overcoming denial. Finally, it is a celebration of perseverance and the slow hard work to recovery.

Martin, Ann M.
A Corner of the Universe
Scholastic, 2002   Grades 5–8
mental illness, obsession, suicide

Twelve-year-old Hattie lives with her parents in their big and once-elegant boardinghouse. She enjoys the boarders, the sleepy upstate New York, 1950s lifestyle, and the summer excitement when the circus comes to town. This is the summer when Hattie's mysterious uncle Adam arrives in town. He moves in with her wealthy grandparents, and comfortable family ties become strained. Hattie's mother avoids her grandparents and won't share information about Uncle Adam's past. It is well into the story that the reader learns that Adam is home because the mental institution where he has lived is closing. Adam is a young man who is childishly exuberant and temperamental. Yet he can glower and burn like a short fuse. Hattie adores her uncle but is unable to protect him from her grandparents' expectations or his own emotional instability. This story reveals the loneliness of mental illness and the emotional stress it places on family; it also illustrates the gift of kindness and acceptance toward those who are different.

Dessen, Sarah
Dreamland: A Novel
Viking, 2000   Grades 8–12
denial, self-esteem, abuse

The story of a teen relationship that turns physically abusive. Caitlin is a fine young woman, but her relationship with Rogerson is flawed. Caitlin's lack of self-worth and her sense of shame, while unhealthy, are all too typical. This story, set against a backdrop of a fun and carefree teen setting, has a scary crack in the mirror. The eventual reflection and resolution is empowering.

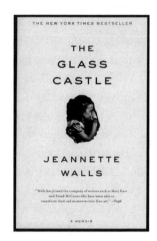

Walls, Jeannette

The Glass Castle: A Memoir

Scribner, 2005   Grade 9–adult
dysfunctional family, mental illness; memoir

Parents Rex and Rose Mary give new meaning to the term *free spirit*. Rex is one creative man. Problem is, he's steeped in delusions and alcohol, keeping his family on the skedaddle from bill collectors and child protection agencies. Rose Mary paints a self-indulged rosy picture, awash in excuses, negligence, and devoid of responsibility. They raise their four children in crisis and conflict, living as indigents without electricity, running water, or adequate heat, food, or shelter. The children bond together and miraculously steer their way through their parents' mayhem. Narrated by their successful journalist daughter, this is a spellbinding adventurous survival tale about afflicted family affections.

Crutcher, Chris

King of the Mild Frontier: An Ill-Advised Autobiography

Greenwillow Books, 2003   Grades 7–12
anger management, addiction; autobiography

Trying to impress the girl of his dreams at a baseball game, young Crutcher—his eye on the gal—gets his teeth batted out. When his big brother says, "Wanna do something neat?" he can't resist. From peeing into the living room space heater to running back and forth like a shooting gallery duck for his brother to take aim with a BB gun, this book answers the rhetorical question, If your brother told you to jump off a bridge, would you do it? Underlying this humorous memoir is Crutcher's mother's battle with alcoholism, his father's overly controlling discipline, and Crutcher's own, very real anger management.

Green, John

Looking for Alaska: A Novel

Dutton Children's Books, 2005   Grade 9–adult
alcoholism, denial, family trauma, death

Sixteen-year-old Miles chronicles his first year at boarding school and the intoxicating infatuation of every temptation it has to offer. Especially the fast, flirty, and unflappable girl of his dreams, Alaska. She is beautiful. She is articulate. She is uninhibited, sophisticated, reckless, adventurous, and yes, self-destructive. This story pulsates with the emotions of teen aspiration, vulnerability, sexuality, and invincibility. On the surface it is all about the young and the restless intellectualizing and philosophizing their way through the pangs of boarding school. Not so surprisingly, in the midst of another drinking bash, Alaska reveals a sad past that she's run from. Despite the tragedy throughout the book, and perhaps because of the teen angst, this smart candid book is one that teens relate to and care about.

Green, John

Paper Towns

Dutton Books, 2008   Grades 8–12
psychological trauma, denial, running away

High school senior Quentin—"Q"—is well adjusted, smart, a band member, and focused on his college aspirations. Well, not entirely. When Quentin was 9 years old, he and his best friend, Margo, discovered a bloody suicide victim sitting under a tree. And so it begins; their lives are irrevocably changed and entangled as they wrestle with the trauma. Margo wildly pushes the envelope to get past the confines of her "paper town." She and Q embark on a nightlong spree to set right all the wrongs in her life. Q, ever cautious about joining her mission, is also ever enthralled with her risky actions. Their 12-hour jaunt is packed with adventurous pranks, all potentially harmful but hilariously fun. Then Margo vanishes, leaving a paper trail of clues behind. Q must reckon with his desire and her ingenious creativity, and at long last, acknowledge her internal conflicts. This powerful story has rich characters and smart teen dialogue. No easy answers or resolutions but a testament to the value of supportive friendships.

Anderson, Laurie Halse
Twisted
Viking, 2007   Grades 7–12
bullying, verbal abuse

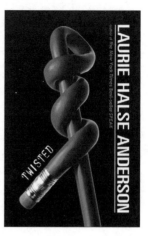

As she did in her Printz Honor winner, *Speak,* Anderson
enters the mind and broken spirit of a senior high school
student—but this time a boy. Tyler must contend with
his mistakes, compounded by a tyrannically obsessive
control-freak father and torqued further by the flirtatious
advances of a rich and manipulative classmate. Tyler's
reactionary dark and dangerous side is tempered and
rectified through self-reflection and resolution. A teen winner with profanity and
sexuality—*start* this as a read-aloud and watch it become an independent read.

NOTES
1. Alison Follos, "Author Profile: The 3 C's of Chris Crutcher," *Library Media Connection* 25, no.
   3 (November/December 2006): 42.
2. Laurie Halse Anderson, AASL author speech, Charlotte, NC, November 2009.
3. ———, interview with the author, November 2009.
4. Follos, "The 3 C's of Chris Crutcher," 41.
5. Laurie Halse Anderson, visit with the author, North Country School, Lake Placid, NY, 2010.
6. Chris Crutcher, "I Don't Give a Damn 'bout My Reputation," *The Book Standard/Kirkus
   Reviews Online*, October 1, 2005.

Stories That Help Us
Surmount the Challenges

Physical and Psychological Illnesses and Accidents

Who knows why some of us are lucky enough to be born with all our fingers, toes, and the ability to stretch our limbs and to see, hear, scream, and move at will through our daily activities. Too many people don't experience these habits and ordinary reflexes. As 15-year-old Elisa, born with cerebral palsy, explains, "I'm always so busy because everything takes me longer. Brushing my teeth takes me longer than it takes my brothers. It is not easy. I have to jump through hoops every day just to get through every day." For children born with disabilities or who have been afflicted with a disability from a very young age, navigating through the everyday world is harder.

The following stories highlight protagonists who live with daily obstacles, whether their own disability or the misconceptions from others about their capabilities. These are also stories about siblings who live with a special needs individual and who learn to balance the expectations of self and family. These stories are selected foremost to attract the reader, to showcase inspirational characters, and to present eye-opening content that is typically overlooked.

I don't pretend to know what will resonate for individual readers dealing with different special needs. I do know that adults sometimes miss the mark of what appeals to children and young adult readers. For example, Ben Mikaelsen's *Petey* is based on a true story of a man with cerebral palsy during the 1920s. It is a book that I had a very difficult time reading, finding it depressing and slow. Yet Elisa calls it one of her favorite books. She says, "I liked *Petey* because it's about someone like me. I understood what Petey was going through. He was called an idiot and I know how that feels—not that I think I'm an idiot! This book was different. Petey was put into a home, and it showed what it was like to be a grownup with CP and how adults treat you." She continues, "People come in and out of his life. It's all very sad." Elisa's reaction makes my opinion of the book inconsequential. Elisa is not saddled in self-pity. She also likes Stephanie Meyer's Twilight series, Nicholas Sparks novels, and *Rules*. About *Rules*, Elisa quips, "No toys in the fish tank!" and flashes an impish smile.

The goal here is to include readable stories that resonate with others, coax an empathetic reaction, encourage awareness and acceptance, and connect readers with different perspectives and life-altering experiences.

Children Coping with Debilitating Accidents, Illness, and Grief

There's no insurance against an accident. Accidents can take away "normal" life in a heartbeat. If you've never lived through a debilitating accident, it's incomprehensible to know what that feels like, let alone the drive such victims must summon to move forward. While nobody wants to belabor the downside of this reality, it is valuable for students to understand what it is like in the body of their physically challenged peers, or simply put, for the physically capable to see past the limitations of their own gifts.

For the recovering accident victim, books that offer escape, solace, and strength are a wise choice. Individual assessment of the reader, particularly if they are recovering from an accident or recent crisis, is important. What are they ready to face or willing to face? Or, just as important, what do they wish to escape? These are all sensitive questions to address before recommending certain titles. In many cases it comes down to teasing out what a person may be seeking but is unable to articulate.

Eighteen-year-old college freshman Terry Fox ignored the pain in his knee. He pushed himself to work very hard to stay on the basketball team. In *Terry Fox: His Story*, one of Fox's teammates remarked, "There were more-talented players who didn't make [the team] . . . but Terry out-gutted them. People tend to look in awe at players who have a lot of natural ability, but respect from other athletes goes to the guy who works really hard, that was Terry." By February, four months later, Terry was diagnosed with osteogenic sarcoma—the most common primary cancer to the bone—and a few weeks later, his leg was amputated. When a basketball coach came to visit Terry in the hospital, he awkwardly brought him a copy of *Runner's World* magazine featuring a story about an amputee who ran the NYC marathon. In Fox's biography, he commented, "It was an impossible dream, a fantasy. That's what it was . . . I was lying in bed looking at this magazine, thinking if he can do it, I can do it too. All it was was an impossibility, something that somebody else does. It was a dream . . . I didn't know if I'd ever walk again." The magazine story stuck with Terry. He couldn't shake it, and it prodded him to take on the impossible: running across Canada and raising money for cancer research. "When I decided to do it, I knew I was going to go all out. There was no in-between."[1] Terry ran the near equivalent of a marathon—daily—for 143 days and raised $24 million dollars for cancer. His too-short life has been celebrated and memorialized. Who knows what it might have been if people looked the other way? If he hadn't read the story that set him on the path of his dream?

In the recommendations in this chapter, protagonists face challenges and inspire pursuance against the odds. Titles that offer motivation for all. Some deal with managing disabilities from birth, others from coping with illnesses, and still others from therapy and rehab recovery after accidents. Many of these stories spark the universal language of spirit, celebrating the will to achieve and to fight the fight. These stories reiterate what Helen Keller said so well: "It is the secret inner will that controls one's fate."[2]

Just to Make Things Trickier: Becoming a Teenager

With the developmental changes of children into teens, there comes an additional emotional challenge: social acceptance. Sally (not her real name), a freshman who wore hearing aids from the time she was 2 years old, wrote about Marlee Matlin's *Deaf Child Crossing*. Sally was surprised that the character in Matlin's novel had similar painful experiences to hers. Sally candidly admitted to relating to the character's fear that people were talking about her behind her back, coping with the mean things that kids said to her face, and wondering about what her life might be like if she didn't have hearing aids. In elementary school a girl had told Sally, "What in the world are those stupid-looking things in your ears? They look funny and dumb—no wonder people think you're a huge, stupid freak." Now older and more confident (though her hearing aids are too conveniently "lost" much of the time), Sally realizes that other kids go through similar challenges. She said she loved Matlin's novel because it helped her realize the "inner me."

Books like *Deaf Child Crossing* reveal the person who may be overshadowed by their disability. Such stories don't ignore differences but promote awareness of the commonalities that we share: the need for friendship, acceptance, and perhaps most of all, visibility. Elisa's mother reminds me, "She would love to have friends with girls her age, and she notices that she doesn't. She told me, 'Sometimes I feel invisible.'"

Elisa's father says, "She loves theater. When she helps out here at the community theater they give her small tasks to do, handing out the programs, taking tickets. That's not what she loves about theater. At the summer camp she went to for disabled children, the kids were all involved, singing, dancing, having a great time. Even if they couldn't make a sound, they were up onstage and part of the show. They were happy. They were included." Being included sounds so simple, but for children with special needs, it can be complicated. Stories that speak to the disability, disorder, dysfunction, and the struggles that set children apart from their contemporaries are a step to repairing the separation. Nothing will magically wipe away the challenges, but stories connect people, lending honor and dignity to our differences. They validate that being different can be a strength, not a weakness.

As with most stories that introduce readers to diverse behaviors and lifestyles, they need a delivery. Oftentimes children and teens want to read for escape. That's great, and it's a necessary tonic for readers needing a break from their own reality. But to help readers identify with a special needs classmate or become empathetic to the diverse learning abilities that surround them, it's important to stock your shelves with a diverse selection of stories. And there are plenty of good ones. Calling attention to people with disabilities is not to pity, exploit, or give undue attention; it is to acknowledge, include, and respect.

Keep in mind that some children and teens contending with a traumatic reality may not be ready for realistic literature. They might benefit from soothing escape reading. There are so many wonderful books to choose from. Harry Potter remains a series that readers enjoy many times over. The late Brian Jacques's Redwall series (twenty-one books in the series!) has many followers and makes a strong connection with fantasy buffs. Fantasy titles are saturating the market, and there are many stories that put readers in charge against evil forces and in control of their destiny. Such titles are not the focus of this book but are readily found in fantasy and sci-fi resources. Keep in mind that bookstores keep these genres shelved separately so they're easy to browse through.

Recent Stumbles

It continues to embarrass me how out of touch, unaware, and insensitive I am to what goes on around me. At the 2011 National Book Festival I rode a shuttle bus with a man who pointed to my wrist, miming for the time. I explained, "It's a bracelet, not a watch." He looked at me, pointed to his ear, and mouthed, "I'm deaf." After my initial discomfort, everything that I had been reading and writing about in this book goaded me not to nod and turn away. Instead, in a moment of clarity, I pulled out my cell phone and shared the digital time display—otherwise, the phone was a useless gadget for him.

Later on, he pantomimed the number 1 and pointed toward his wrist. I was perplexed and he repeated the gesture several times. Miserably, I failed to understand and with resignation, he turned away. Later, while walking through the tent-land of book events along the National Mall I saw a sign with the day's posted schedule: "Sunday, 1:00–5:00 P.M." What he had been trying to tell me was so obvious—the event opened at one o'clock! It struck me how removed and disconnected we are without our traditional anchors—in this case, verbal communication. If communication isn't delivered in a familiar manner, our brains stumble about awkwardly, incapable of "getting it." Learning a little ASL in public schools makes sense. Twenty-four years ago my daughter, Caroline, befriended a deaf student in her fourth-grade classroom. Caroline learned ASL alongside her deaf classmate. This carried on through fifth grade. Recently Caroline called me to say, "Mom, I waited on two deaf diners last evening, and it was amazing how I was able to sign with them. It all came back!" While you may never have a reason to use classroom foreign language skills, it is probable that you will have an opportunity to communicate in ASL.

The influence of Brian Selznick's awe-inspiring book *Wonderstruck*—a book with two deaf protagonists on parallel adventures—made a notable ripple at the National Book Festival. Book-signing tents lined one promenade of the Mall while hordes of book-clutching people extended toward the grassy center. One line extended serpentine-like, with seven links of close to a hundred people in each section. It was a hot day, and *Wonderstruck*—in all its awesome glory—is a big and heavy book. Lugging three copies stacked under other authors' titles is an armload. The lines moved slowly, and restless adults sent misery texts to bide time and vent frustration. But here's the thing: children plopped down on the grass, opened *Wonderstruck,* and oblivious to discomfort, heat, or time, they sank into the story and blissfully faded away.

Brian Selznick is a family descendant of David O. Selznick, who produced many movies, including *Gone with the Wind* and *Rebecca.* Brian is also the descendant of the silent movie industry distributor Lewis J. Selznick. These relations directly and indirectly influence Brian Selznick's work. He is visually creative, his illustrations purposefully zoom in and out like a camera lens, and he is sensitive to the notion that "deaf people are a people of the eye."[3] In *Wonderstruck* there's a scene of the advent of the talking movie, and thus the end of the silent film industry. Like a door slammed shut, deaf people were excluded from a previously more inclusive and popular mode of entertainment. Everything about *Wonderstruck* appeals to the eye, and by default, the deaf. At his National Book Festival presentation, Selznick was joined by his brother, who is deaf in one ear like the main character in *Wonderstruck.* Through his brother, Selznick learned about the communication difficulties his characters would encounter. Selznick's speech was simultaneously presented by an American Sign Language interpreter. In fact, all of the author presentations at the 2011 National Book Festival were accompanied by ASL interpreters. We are all capable of reaching out, taking a moment to assist, to acknowledge, and to consider the gaps, however uncontrollable, in our differences.

Organizations like the Library of Congress are doing their part. They are the backbone of the National Book Festival and are genuine advocates for people with special needs. In addition to the ASL interpreters for author presentations, an accessibility and information tent offered access to ASL interpreters, assistive learning devices (ALDs), large-print programs, and Braille programs.

Suggested Reading

PHYSICAL, PSYCHOLOGICAL, AND EMOTIONAL
DISABILITIES, AND MEDICAL ILLNESS

Alexie, Sherman
The Absolutely True Diary
of a Part-Time Indian
Little, Brown, 2007 Grades 9–12
hydrocephalus, racial conflict, dysfunctional family

In this book based on the author's life, 14-year-old Arnold was born with water on the brain (hydrocephalus) and was homeschooled for the beginning of his elementary school years. He read incessantly to help pass the time and became the wicked-smart teen who is out of sync at his Spokane Indian reservation school. Determined to secure a better education and escape the rez, Arnold commutes to the "white school." He's accepted as much as a curiosity as a new, smart, dorky kid. But he's now alienated himself from the folks on the reservation, including his best friend. With a masterful droll tone and an unfailing ability to draw readers into his story, Sherman creates a powerful and bittersweet sketch of overcoming personal adversity. The slight graphic novel format invites reluctant readers into a compellingly readable story.

Matlin, Marlee
Deaf Child Crossing
Simon & Schuster Books for Young Readers, 2002 Grades 3–6
hearing impairment

The Oscar-winning actress writes about a topic she knows well—the difficulties of growing up deaf. Nine-year-old Megan is excited when Cindy moves in. Megan is outgoing and friendly; Cindy is shy and a bit introverted. Megan is deaf; Cindy can hear. They are both likeable young characters that form an unlikely best friendship. When Megan makes a new friend at deaf camp, there's tension in Megan and Cindy's friendship. How they resolve their hurt feelings is the stuff that monopolizes 9-year-old girls' lives. This slight, light novel is a great choice for all young girls.

Paulsen, Gary

The Monument

Delacorte Press, 1991   Grades 6–9
physical disability, adoption

Even getting her hair just so and wearing a new dress, 9-year-old Rocky figures nobody wants to adopt a caramel-colored-skin kid with a leg brace. She figures wrong and ends up in the care of a kind, indulgent, if somewhat preoccupied older alcoholic couple. Rocky then rescues a troublesome stray dog that becomes her fierce companion and her compass toward adventure. They in turn befriend Mick, a vagabond artist commissioned to design a war memorial in the community. Mick is a hard-drinking cross between bum and free-spirited visionary. Under his tutelage Rocky emerges from shy observer to confident, expressive artist. She discovers her personal strengths and becomes aware of superficial weaknesses. Rocky finds the good and becomes open to experience the exciting. Once again Paulsen deserves his unshakable reputation as a wonderful storyteller. In Rocky he's created an intelligent girl with a humble manner and a sharp and exacting eye for truth.

Matlin, Marlee, and Doug Cooney

Nobody's Perfect

Simon and Schuster Books for Young Readers, 2006   Grades 4–6
autism, hearing impairment

Megan is excited about her upcoming purple birthday party. She is inviting every fourth-grade girl in her class and has doted over her purple-sparkle-and-feather-bedecked invitations. When the new girl, Alexis, arrives in town, there's suddenly a fly in the ointment. Should Megan invite her or not? So begins the dilemma.

     Megan is deaf and is familiar with challenges. She takes on problems with a no-nonsense maturity. When Alexis rebuffs her overtures of friendship, Megan is irritated but not destroyed. Megan is perturbed, not because she's deaf but because Alexis acts aloof.

Megan is a typical kid. Being deaf is part of the many pieces of who she is. Her disability is annoying when she's unable to read people's lips—if they speak too fast or they turn their backs. Especially aggravating is trying to read her friend's lips, her pink braces stuffed with food pieces. Gross!

When her teacher teams Megan and Alexis up for the science experiment contest, some of the chilly barriers begin to dissolve. They test the waters of their friendship, and while that becomes stronger, Alexis's mysterious behaviors continue to crop up. Why won't she invite Megan to her house? Why won't she attend Megan's birthday party? When Megan learns more about Alexis's family, things begin to make sense. A good choice for young readers to view the reality and the normalcy of living in a special needs family.

Brooks, Martha
Queen of Hearts
Farrar, Straus and Giroux, 2011   Grades 7–10
tuberculosis, family illness, sanatorium

It is 1941 when almost-16-year-old Marie-Claire's life is blown to smithereens: she and her siblings contract tuberculosis. She is also sick with guilt over sneaking out to visit their uncle in the TB sanatorium. She is certain this is why her little brother, Luc, is stricken with illness. Luc has been coughing and is frail. He is failing fast, yet it is months before he, their littler sister, and Marie-Claire are diagnosed with the dreaded disease. They are sent from home to chase the cure at the sanatorium in Manitoba, the very place their uncle died, a veritable community of hospital wards, sleeping porches, and cure cottages. Marie-Claire, feeling tired all the time, is confined to her bed for physical rest and the hope that the lesions on her lung will heal. Her roommate, Signy, is a rich city girl who has lived at the sanatorium in the clutches of TB for way too many

Additional Titles of Interest Featured in Other Chapters

years. Signy receives many gifts but few family visits. She is timid, kind, and desperate to befriend the querulous and gruff- mannered Marie-Claire. Being bedridden does little to snuff Marie-Claire's feisty spirit. She is prodded, x-rayed, forced to endure painful medical procedures—including a surgically induced collapsed lung—and humiliatingly dependent on nurses with bedpans, who wheel her out onto the freezing porch to sleep bundled up for the "Klondike" treatment. Marie-Claire and her fellow young patients are shortchanged out of living at home, going to school, flirting with the soldiers at community dances, and taking their youth for granted.

The mysterious TB disease struck young and old. Some fought and won, some succumbed—the way to beat it seemed as mystical as the illness itself. The lives of the residents in the sanatorium—a small, self-sufficient city of sorts—animate this story with fascinating historical and medical detail and make you want to know more.

Alexander, Sally Hobart, and Robert Alexander

She Touched the World:
Laura Bridgman, Deaf-Blind Pioneer

Clarion Books, 2008   Grades 4–12

blindness, deafness, mutism

This picture book is saturated with historical information about Laura Bridgman, a deaf, blind, and mute child who fought her way out of sensory isolation. Laura lived during the 1800s and was one of the first students in the first school for the blind, eventually known as Perkins School for the Blind. Laura had scarlet fever as a little girl, and while she lost two sisters to the disease, she survived. However, she lost her hearing, eyesight, voice, sense of smell, and ability to taste. Surrounded by a large farm family yet unable to communicate, she was confined to loneliness. Almost serendipitously, it was a young Dartmouth student helping to settle the town's tax bills who became enthralled with Laura's curiosity. He called Laura to the attention of his professor. Thus began the fortuitous connections that were to help Laura unlock her confinement. She spent much of her young life at the Perkins School for the Blind, where she learned to fingerspell, read, and write. (One of her teachers was Anne Sullivan, who became synonymously known with the famous Helen Keller.) This story is fascinating in describing the medical difficulties Laura Bridgman overcame, the rare accomplishments she achieved, and the hope that she inspires. It is worth noting that the author Sally Hobart Alexander became blind at age 27.

Crutcher, Chris
Staying Fat for Sarah Byrnes
Greenwillow Books, 1993   Grades 8–12
disfigurement, psychological trauma, abuse

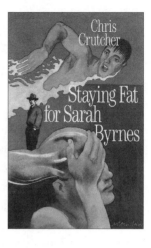

Caught in the grip of the mean junior high years, Eric, an overweight social misfit, and his best friend, Sarah Byrnes, disfigured from a childhood accident, are a supportive and likeable twosome. The story follows them through high school, where Eric participates in competitive swimming, slims down, and gains self-confidence. Meanwhile, Sarah's mysterious life goes from worse to dangerous. When she stops talking and is committed to a mental ward, Eric risks their friendship by divulging her secrets to enlist support. Like a scary chess game, malevolent acts from dangerous adults threaten both teens. Another one of Crutcher's pitch-perfect stories, with suspense, drama, heroic protagonists, adversity, advocacy, and best of all, resolution.

Hayes, Daniel
The Trouble with Lemons
D. R. Godine, 1991   Grades 6–9
asthma, death, bullying, psychological trauma

Swimming smack into a dead body takes the fun out of two boys' innocent late-night dip in a quarry. Tyler has hyper-allergies, and a severe asthma attack can kill him. Triggers include food, plants, fear, and panic. He keeps a low profile and tries to avoid stressful situations. He is just getting over the death of his father. Needless to say, the evening at the quarry is bad for his health. With strong suspicions about who the murderer is, Tyler must overcome his fear of confrontation and notify the police. Witty dialogue and self-deprecating teen humor contribute to this page-turning mystery.

Berg, Elizabeth
We Are All Welcome Here: A Novel
Ballantine, 2007   Grade 7—adult
polio, codependence, racial conflict

In this book based on a true story, 14-year-old Diana and her beautiful mother, Paige, who is paralyzed from polio, are a captivating duo. Peacie, the black caregiver and Paige's right-hand lady, makes three: she's an integral member of this intrepid team. Young Diana, with her mother anchored to a bed, has freedom and independence. She experiences typical teen angst and suffers fits of vexation from Peacie's protective interference. Paige is a woman whose moxie and beauty outshine her disability at every turn. How Paige, physically powerless but emotionally powerful, successfully raises, controls, and influences her adolescent daughter is fascinating. Peacie's roles as protector, provider, and proctor keep the family intact. Paige is vital and inspirational, and polio is a lifelong obstacle that she confronts as a daily routine. The scary battle hovers in the wings, the 1964 civil rights movement, which for Paige is the fight to win. Diana learns to admire both Paige and Peacie, especially her mother's captivity within her body and her amazing inner vitality to prevail. Even Peacie's annoying bossiness is forgiven due to her unwavering devotion. And as expected with three women in a household, there are the men who touch their lives. An inspirational and heartening story that resonates in credibility, tone, and the intrinsic value of human decency. (One of my favorite books!)

Monninger, Joseph
Wish
Delacorte Press, 2010   Grades 6–9
cystic fibrosis

Eleven-year-old Tommy is fascinated with sharks. His seemingly infinite knowledge of shark facts eclipses his captivity by cystic fibrosis. Tommy spends little time focused on his illness; sharks are where it's at. Often struggling for breath, an inhaler always nearby, he periodically wears an electric vest to jiggle free the settled gunk in his lungs. His 15-year-old sister, Bee, who mostly takes care of him, and his single mom, who mostly doesn't, join him on a sponsored trip to California. Bee is Tommy's heroine. She is smart and attentive and will do anything to increase the quality of Tommy's life, including going on a shark-sighting boat trip. The reality of how fragile life is, how tenuous relationships are, and how everything is not as simple as it appears makes up much of this story. Not letting physical/medical disabilities control your passion is the rest.

ACCIDENT AND SUDDEN ILLNESS

Cushman, Karen

Alchemy and Meggy Swann

Clarion Books, 2010   Grades 4–7
physical disability; historical novel

Meggy Swann masters the use of her walking sticks—stick, swing, drag—as she navigates through the slimy streets of London. Meggy has been turned out by her mother and sent to live with the father she's never met. He ignores her presence, the house is cold and filthy, and there is no food or money. Along with her only companion—a cantankerous goose called Louise—Meggy takes up with a bohemian family. She is embraced by this free-spirited group of artists, street musicians, and performers.

Meggy is a stalwart and courageous 14-year-old. While her legs always hurt and hamper her every move, they never get the best of her. Her spirit shines through the tumult of 1573 London, where poverty, bogus laws, ignorance, and brutal acts of historical notoriety abound. Meanwhile, Meggy's father is possessed with a mission to conjure concoctions in a mad attempt to turn ordinary metals into gold. Fueled by the necessity of funding his obsession, he sells poison to scheming men. Meggy is determined to thwart the malevolent plans, even if it means destroying her father. Her matter-of-fact behavior and forthright determination are the alchemy that transforms lame legs into an endearing and strong character. You won't feel sorry for Meggy Swann!

Cummings, Priscilla

Blindsided

Dutton Children's Books, 2010   Grades 7–9
blindness, visual impairment

Fourteen-year-old Natalie's future is becoming dimmer, as the loss of her eyesight is a nightmare she can't avoid. As she states, "You can't prepare for going blind." From the age of eight, Natalie's vision has been diminishing from a congenital disease. This beautiful, smart, well-grounded teen is panicked by her loss and humiliated by being seen as different. Part of going from denial to acceptance is attending a boarding school for the blind. She concentrates on learning Braille, using her despised cane, taking self-defense classes, making new friends (and trying not to mourn the loss of her old ones). She aches to remain normal and inconspicuous.

This story rattles the complacency of the simple gifts of physical normalcy and brings awareness to the tremendous barriers the blind face, visible and otherwise. Natalie is a credible character, and her fear is palpable and painful. The story rushes to a climax of high drama and action as Natalie's emotional battles turn outward, from melodramatic boarding school life—roommate trouble, tragedy, vulnerable blind girls attacked by drunks—to tending the family farm in her parents' absence when everything goes wrong. At times the all-at-once action is over the top, but young readers will enjoy the tension and Natalie's potential capabilities.

Sachar, Louis

The Cardturner

Delacorte Press, 2010   Grades 8–12

blindness, diabetes, mental illness

Alton is his Uncle Trapp's "eyes," aka his cardturner, during Trapp's bridge tournaments. The elderly Trapp, severely diabetic and blind, is a world-class master bridge player with a sharp wit and cantankerous personality. He is intense, no-nonsense, and demanding, with bridge and in life. Alton watches carefully and begins to learn the art of the game. The two form what appears to be an opportunistic and unlikely relationship. While Trapp depends on Alton to drive him to the bridge games and "read" the cards, he does nothing to show his appreciation. For all the respect that Alton has toward his uncle's mastery, he's peeved that his uncle questions his motives and assumes the worst about his intelligence. Alton stifles his annoyance. He covers his guilt and disgust over his parents' insufferable greed—they want Alton to butter up the old guy so they'll inherit his oodles of cash. Enter Toni, the cute and slightly nuts granddaughter of Trapp's long-dead bridge partner. Set against the complicated game of bridge is the clever, character-driven tale of good kids and flawed adults. As Alton unravels Trapp's history, the story becomes entangled with drama, spiritual mystery, and tragic romance. Gifted storyteller Louis Sachar does a smooth job of grabbing your attention, testing your concentration, and breathing soul into the intergenerational bonds of family.

Green, John
The Fault in Our Stars
Dutton Books, 2012   Grades 9–12
cancer

Seventeen-year-old Hazel Grace was diagnosed with thyroid cancer at 13. After radical surgery, radiation, and multiple cancer drugs, the stubborn tumors on her lungs remain. But thus far, a miracle drug stems their growth.

Protected and housebound, Hazel Grace has not been to school in three years. She is shy, observant, and intelligent. She is also jaded and depressed, and rightfully so. She totes an oxygen tank and nose nubbins everywhere she goes, and still she fights for breath. While this story does not ignore Hazel's fragility, it is less about illness and more about falling out of depression and into love. Hazel's lungs may falter, but her quick wit and candid nature kindle a fast attraction with the intuitive and sexy Augustus, whom she meets at a cancer support group. Gus is a former basketball star who lost a leg to osteosarcoma. Living with the gift of remission, he is ever social and dynamic. He pursues Hazel Grace with a single focus and wins her over with his funny, smart, and confident personality.

Before there was Augustus, Hazel's intellectual passion was centered on a novel and its elusive author—an obsession that leads the young couple on a trip to Amsterdam.

Additional Titles of Interest Featured in Other Chapters

Their story becomes a metaphor of the elusive search for closure and the futile attempt to control destiny—one's own as well as another's. Teens will be hooked by their selfless, heroic romance. This tragic story is a beautiful testament of the precarious, unpredictable, yet inevitable pages and stages of life. Hazel Grace and Augustus Waters are spirited paper characters contributing to the infinite universe of great lives in literature.

Lawlor, Laurie
Helen Keller: Rebellious Spirit
Holiday House, 2001   Grades 6–12
blindness, deafness, speech problems

A biography that underscores the vitality, vigilance, and determination necessary to take life by the horns and make it your own. This book highlights Helen's brilliance as well as her resolute tenacity. Her story is inspirational for those who are living without sight or hearing or who have difficulty speaking, as well as for those who are blessed with all five senses. For those who have been waiting on the sidelines, her story is a kick in the butt. Helen lived during a time when being blind, deaf, and mute was viewed as a social and cultural stigma. Many disabled people were put away in asylums. Helen was not a little girl to be ignored; fortunately her mother, while helpless to reach her, felt a flicker of something special in Helen and would not consider putting her away.

As a child Helen demanded attention and behaved in a spoiled and feral way. Her behavior was an instinctual effort to communicate. Helen's good fate was the young teacher, Anne Sullivan, also partially blind, arriving from the Perkins Institution for the Blind to teach Helen. (Their story has been immortalized in the play *The Miracle Worker*; see chapter 3, p. 29.) At first it was a battle of the wills, but fortunately Anne wasn't easily thwarted. She gave Helen the gift of language, teaching her to fingerspell into her palm. Helen's quest for knowledge, her passion for human equality, and her enthusiasm for companionship were set free. She attended Radcliffe, and with Anne as her personal interpreter, she graduated without additional assistance. She mastered Braille and later worked diligently to support one Braille style (at one time there were five!). She became famous for her intelligence as well as her political and social activism. She wrote to one teacher, "When I came to your class last October, I was trying with all my might to be like everybody else, to forget as entirely as possible my limitations' peculiar environment. Now, however, I see the folly of attempting to hitch one's wagon to a star that does not belong to it. . . . Henceforth I am resolved to be myself, to live my own life, and write my own thoughts when I have any" (p. 88). While *The Miracle Worker* is a fine introduction to Helen's story, her later accomplishments are well represented in this easy-to-comprehend, intriguing biography.

Paulsen, Gary

Notes from the Dog

Wendy Lamb Books, 2009   Grades 6–12

phobia, emotional disability, cancer

Fourteen-year-old Finn can count his friends on one hand. He's terrified of meeting new people, and conversation is painful. His best friend, Matthew, is talkative, overly confident and sometimes a thorn in Finn's side. Finn's contentment comes from books and his dog, Dylan. He's determined that his summer vacation will not be marred by the intrusion of people and the discomfort they cause.

Finn meets his pretty new neighbor, 20-something Johanna, an exuberant woman who shares her joy of life while facing down its untimely end. Johanna employs Finn to help her create gardens in a sorrowful-looking backyard. Johanna's enthusiasm for research, compost, fertilizer, and all things dirt break down Finn's barriers. Before he knows it, he's dug deep into Johanna's garden project.

When Johanna tells the boys that she is a breast cancer survivor their initial trepidation shifts to protective friendship. They earnestly help her through the messy aftermath of chemo treatments. Johanna's spirit and optimism infuse Finn with courage and love. Told with Paulsen's signature humor and hard-hitting candor, this tender tale is a salute to the bravest of brave.

Mikaelsen, Ben

Petey

Hyperion Books for Children, 1998   Grades 7–12

cerebral palsy, physical deformity, mental disability

Based on a true story. Petey was born with cerebral palsy in the 1920s. His limbs won't unfold or grow properly—he is folded in on himself, his wrists bent back, his legs pulled up, and his tongue gnarled so he can barely speak or eat properly. At age 2 he was misdiagnosed as "retarded" and put into an insane asylum to live for the next several decades. But Petey is not the "idiot" that he has been labeled. He begins to have meaningful relationships with his caregivers. He is also befriended by Calvin, who has a clubfoot, is developmentally delayed, and becomes seriously depressed within their horrific surroundings. Petey's is a sad story of life imprisoned by the body—and institutionalized by others. Often Petey's life is devoid of any attentive kindness. At story's end Petey is elderly, and it is a young teen who reaches beyond his own apprehension to become Petey's advocate.

It was painful for me to read about a victim of CP who is a victim of institutional misdiagnosis and abuse. Having said that, two teens—one who has cerebral palsy and one who doesn't—told me that this was one of their favorite books, and so I include it here.

Byars, Betsy

The Pinballs

Harper and Row, 1977   Grades 5–8
accident, neglect, abandonment, abuse, orphanhood, foster care

You would never think that kids lumped together because of lousy parenting would make such an entertaining story. Carlie, Harvey, and Thomas J have landed in foster care—randomly placed together with the kind Mason couple. The kids are not related and are as different as they could be. Harvey's father accidentally ran over his legs; Dad was a little too drunk and a lot too preoccupied missing the wife who left him. With two broken legs, Harvey is anchored to his wheelchair, reliving his broken home life. Thomas J is quiet and shy. He was abandoned as a baby and left in the driveway of the elderly Benson twins, who neglected to report him. They've raised him until now, when broken 86-year-old twin hips put them in the hospital and Thomas J in foster care. Carlie has good reason to be suspicious of life and everyone around her. She's not missing stepfather No. 2, who physically attacked her. He wasn't much better than stepfather No. 1, who did the same, or even her dad, who abandoned Mom before Carlie was born. Mom is a shadow, unable—or incapable—of protecting her daughter.

The very caring Mr. and Mrs. Mason provide Carlie and the boys plenty of space for healing. Carlie is one tough cookie; a cynical viewpoint and a sarcastic tone are her armor. She loves drama and being the center of attention, and her snide quips and mean retorts take center stage. When she's not annoying the boys, she riles and rallies them. For all her grousing she puts her willfulness to positive good, and when Harvey ends up back in the hospital, it is Carlie who is determined to revive his broken spirit. This is one slight story with a jab that hits the heart: good kids can have bad parents. Yet for young readers in tough spots, it's reaffirming to know that they're not alone and that outside their rotten homes, care and kindness do exist.

Dorris, Michael
Sees behind Trees
Hyperion Books for Children, 1996   Grades 3–9
visual impairment

A nearsighted Native American boy tries to excel in his tribal traditions and take part in rites of passage—in particular, developing skill using the bow and arrow. For the visually impaired youth, this is an exercise in frustration. His sympathetic uncle invents a new challenge, "to see what can't be seen." Honing his senses, he develops self-confidence and succeeds in unexpected ways.

Park, Linda Sue
A Single Shard
Clarion Books, 2001   Grades 4–8
orphanhood, homelessness, physical disability, death

In this 2002 Newbery Award winner, Park re-creates the Korean ancient lifestyle of a twelfth-century pottery apprentice and his wise caregiver. The novel is rich with overcoming adversity, proceeding with tenacity, and pushing past obstacles. Crane-man, hobbled by a shriveled leg, is raising a 10-year-old orphan, Tree-ear. The two live under a bridge, where they survive on rubbish and rice grains. They are poor, hungry, and homeless, but Crane-man teaches Tree-ear the value of relationships, philosophical wisdom, and respectful moral behaviors. The struggling pair are rich in selfless kindness. When Tree-ear embarks on a quest to secure a commission for the potter's work, his physical and emotional mettle are tested; his sustaining fortitude comes from Crane-man's tutelage. This is an adventurous historical novel that focuses on the enduring strengths of care and love instead of the limits of doubt and physical disabilities.

Holt, Kimberly Willis

When Zachary Beaver Came to Town

Holt, 1999   Grades 5–8

obesity, friendship

Toby's mom leaves a big hole in his life when she goes off to become a music star in Nashville. Toby and his best buddy, Cal, pass their time in the sleepy summertime heat of their hometown of Antler, Texas. Cal's big brother, Wayne, off fighting in Vietnam, also leaves a hole. Mom and Wayne stay in touch through their letters home. Toby stashes Mom's letters, unopened, on his dresser. The boys eagerly await Wayne's, read them together, and hear his longing for Antler. He makes it sound like paradise.

Zachary Beaver shows up in town as a freakish carnival act, pulled by a pint-size travel trailer with a manager barking tickets to see "the fattest boy in the world." Toby and Cal are unprepared for the sight of the 600-plus-pound Zachary or the conflicting emotions that meeting his hostile gaze stirs. Zachary is left behind in Antler by his manager. He knows no one and is trapped in the trailer that he fills. Barely able to walk or support his own weight, fed and entrapped by a culture's fascination for misfortune, Zachary Beaver is hidden by a lifetime of being looked at, ridiculed, and exploited.

After Toby's mind-set shifts during another encounter with "the fat boy," Toby and Cal become the "soldiers" who protect the turtle that Zachary has become. Cal's older, wiser, compassionate sister joins their mission. They coax Zachary out of his shell to go to the drive-in movie. The boys turn from viewing Zachary as a spectacle and begin a tentative friendship. All are forced to peer beyond the self-deception in each of their lives. A terrific story about looking at the entwined hearts and intricate lives that contribute to the complexities of a simple little town.

Palacio, R. J.

Wonder

Alfred A. Knopf, 2012   Grades 5–7

birth defects, reconstructive surgery

Ten-year-old August has always been homeschooled. Born with severe facial deformities, August has had twenty-four operations to restructure a cleft palate, rebuild his nose, and develop nonexistent ear tissue. He's spent more time recovering from his surgeries than playing and growing up like an ordinary kid.

Fifth grade is a scary place for a kid who has never been to school. But it's especially nerve-wracking for a little boy who is stared at everywhere he goes. As he explains, he's "the only kid who looks like me" (p. 12). August is ever resilient from his lifetime of dealing with multiple plastic surgeries. Braving school is going to be a different kind of challenge, but no less difficult.

The kids behave as to be expected; they stare, turn away, or pretend they don't see. Fifth graders can be selfish and heartless. They can also be selfless and honorable. The mean kids target August with their ignorance and cruelty. The nice ones are curious and kind, becoming his allies and champions. They work with him on school projects, invite him to their homes, share laughter, and honestly work at the nuanced bonds of good friendships.

Told through separate narratives, beginning with August's viewpoint, the reader shares August's story through multiple perspectives, from his pretty and well-adjusted sister—who reveals the sacrifices of her parents' attention to the chronic necessities of August's recovery—to their many and various friends.

August's life is undoubtedly difficult; even adults have trouble hiding their shocked response to his disfigurement. But with increased support from those around him, he faces his fear by revealing his face. The experience is tough and challenging, but it is also rich with possibility, refreshingly inspirational, and sometimes even funny.

Selznick, Brian
Wonderstruck: A Novel in Words and Pictures
Scholastic Press, 2011   Grades 4–8
deafness, orphanhood; illustrated

When his mother is killed in a car accident, Ben moves in with his neighboring aunt and uncle. Ben is deaf in one ear, but that's never bothered him much. The death of his mother does. One evening, lonely and longing, Ben is drawn to a light on in his mother's empty cottage bedroom. There he discovers treasures of his mother's life: a tin of saved cash, a jewelry box, a silver locket with a photograph of a young man, an envelope with a mysterious love letter, a telephone number—and a small yellowed illustrated book, *Wonderstruck*. A jolt from a storm shakes him from his mourning and compels him to travel from the natural wilderness of his Minnesota home to follow the hints from his mother's treasures—foremost to track down his father through the chaos of New York City.

In alternate chapters, from fifty years before, a young girl is brought to life through bold and vivid illustrations. Rose is deaf. Her mother, a famous silent movie starlet and her father, a stern and silent doctor, keep Rose safely housebound. Rose wants more than to practice sign language and be trapped in a lonely house. She spends time daydreaming, making paper sculptures of buildings and re-creating miniature paper cities. She sneaks out to the movies—the silent picture shows, where the hearing and the deaf enjoy popular culture equally. She escapes to movies that bring her closer to the glamorous mother who left them for the silver screen and seeks out family who will support her journey to break free from isolation.

Ben's journey to find his mysterious father and Rose's mission to connect with the world are propelled along different tracks toward an intersecting destiny, their paths dovetailing in exceptional ways. This story of adventure, courage, and historical relevance exceeds conventional standards. An inspiring tale of wonder and possibilities, it is also testament to the human spirit, ambition, talent, family connection, tenacity, and the inexplicable power of serendipity. The alternately written and illustrated chapters are a complement of contrasts, different mediums that appeal to different intelligences and diverse senses. Two modes of distinct communication—text and illustration—hinged together, independent, entwined, profound, and thought provoking. *Wonderstruck,* with its intricate story lines and its artful composition, will leave readers with just that feeling.

ACCIDENT VICTIMS AND SUDDEN ILLNESS

Pearson, Mary E.
The Adoration of Jenna Fox
Henry Holt, 2008   Grades 8–12
accident, coma, cloning

A horrific car accident has kept Jenna in a medically induced coma for over a year—or so she's told. The reality is murky, and Jenna begins to suspect that her recovery is laced with something remarkable but questionable. Along with disjointed and troubled memories of the accident are Jenna's increased concerns about her present. What is the truth that her scientist parents seem reluctant to share? This is a fascinating story of a too-good-to-be true situation that showcases issues of cloning and immortality. Is Jenna a captive in her new reality? At least she lives—or *does* she? Suspenseful and thought-provoking, this novel pits miracle against medical ethics.

Sonnenblick, Jordan
After Ever After
Scholastic Press, 2010   Grades 7–12
cancer, friendship

We meet older brother Steven in *Drums, Girls, and Dangerous Pie* (see chapter 7, page 109). This is younger brother Jeffrey's narrative. Jeffrey and Tad have been best friends for years. They begin their eighth-grade year haunted by their medical past. Both are cancer survivors carrying the persistent fear of recurrence. Jeffrey has a slight physical limp and a massive math learning disability, the residual effects from treatments for his childhood leukemia. Tad is in a wheelchair, the result of too many operations and treatments from his three separate bouts with cancer. The boys face new teen-filled challenges in eighth grade: girls, gym, and grades. Their goal? To get to graduation: Jeffrey passing the state math exam and Tad walking. In the background are typical family members with their typical combinations of support and interference. Jeffrey's older brother, Steven, is in Africa finding himself and e-mailing sage—if clichéd—advice back to Jeffrey. Their parents are in a constant state of discord over the anxiety and pressure of the state test on Jeffrey. Tad's battle, kept in the shadows, while no less immediate, is much more serious.

The story celebrates good friendships and loving families as it gently cautions about taking good health and life for granted. Despite the sad reality, which is fairly predictable, there is much teen energy, banter, and humor that makes the story approachable and told without undue drama.

Crutcher, Chris
The Crazy Horse Electric Game
Greenwillow Books, 1987   Grades 8–12
paralysis, physical therapy, speech problems, therapeutic school, Asperger's syndrome

High school junior Willie Weaver suffers a severe head injury in a waterskiing accident. He's lucky to be alive, but he doesn't see it that way. Willie is unable to accept the loss of his athletic skill, his speech difficulty, or anyone's pity. He runs away and lands in the inner city of Oakland, California. After being mugged, beaten, and robbed by a gang, Willie is rescued by a bus driver/pimp who enrolls him in One More Last Chance High School. OMLCHS is a school for teens with special needs, learning disabilities, aptitude problems, or parents who want their children to have more attention than they'd get in the public school. Through the care and attention of the school staff—a combination of teachers, mentors, counselors and physical therapists—Willie regains his mental and physical abilities and his self-confidence. He learns to work hard, let go of the guilt and blame, and reach out to help others. The school is where he meets a most remarkable group of people, from supportive and well-meaning adults to other students whose troubles far exceed his own. Willie faces the crib death of his sister; divorce; drugs; sexual stirrings; gang violence; mental, emotional, and physical handicaps; prostitution; child beating; and more—a lot for one book, let alone one kid. Crutcher is the king of pitting insurmountable physical challenges against unimaginable emotional odds; he pushes the tension and stretches his characters' resilience. For all of Willie's physical challenges, there's an equal amount of self-reflection and recovery.

Dickinson, Peter

Eva

Paw Prints, 2008   Grades 8–12
coma, physical injury; science fiction

After a car accident, 13-year-old Eva is in a coma, her body crushed and almost lifeless. Her scientist parents make the tough decision to allow a medical experiment that will save her. Eva's brain cells are implanted into a chimpanzee's brain; her life goes on in theory and motion, but with unimaginable upsets, conflicts, and consequences. As Eva adjusts to her new life inside a chimpanzee body and within the chimp community, she stays a keen human observer. Nonetheless, she slowly adapts, assuming a chimp's instinctual behaviors and life-sustaining habits. Told from Eva's intelligent perspective, this is a fascinating and suspenseful read. Similar to the crisis and questionable practices of tampering with mortality in *The Adoration of Jenna Fox* (page 74), this story has the humanistic bonus of characters communicating with and developing attachments to a primate tribe.

Additional Titles of Interest Featured in Other Chapters

Hamilton, Scott

The Great Eight: How to Be Happy (Even When You Have Every Reason to Be Miserable)

Thomas Nelson, 2008   Grade 8–adult

childhood illness, cancer; autobiography

Scott Hamilton: an Olympic gold medal figure skating champion, a force that defied nature as he back-flipped his way to skating stardom, the brainchild of the world-famous *Stars on Ice* show, and a dynamic figure skating commentator—his accomplishments are great and varied. This Olympian who excelled at it all was dropped to his knees by unexpected and inexplicable illnesses. Through his daily regime of skating the figure eight—a graphic diagram of precision and perfection—Scott explains how he lives his life through repetition, focus, and personal discipline, providing the fortitude to battle testicular cancer and survive a brain tumor. Physical adversity is nothing new for Scott. He fought a childhood illness that left him forever small in physical stature but fed his fierce drive and optimistic attitude. How he fought back and got up again and again is a study in his willful grit of greatness.

Hamilton, Scott, and Lorenzo Benet

Landing It: My Life On and Off the Ice

Kensington Books, 1999   Grade 8–adult

childhood illness, cancer; autobiography

The life of Olympic figure skating champion Scott Hamilton—from the highs of success to the rock-bottom lows of medical challenge—is something you just can't make up. This is a look at Scott's personal life on and off the ice. From the ages of 3 to 9 years old, Scott had a mysterious physical growth defect: his body would not absorb nutrients, and thus he didn't grow. He spent years in and out of hospitals, on and off diets, in and out of school, and was misdiagnosed many times. Sometimes he was hooked up to IVs to keep him alive. He wasn't playing ball with the rest of the kids on the block. He wasn't playing at all. Finally a doctor refined his diet and told him to go lead a normal life. He had a lot of catching up to do, but with skating, he caught on quickly. It is Scott's fiercely positive belief that everything he's accomplished in skating (and life) is a result of adversity and perseverance. He amassed a slew of figure skating championships, including the gold medal in the 1984 Olympics. In 1990 he was inducted into the US Olympic Hall of Fame, and he continued to win major skating competitions throughout the 1990s. In 1997 Scott was diagnosed with testicular cancer. As of this writing, he has successfully battled four major health assaults, including a serious childhood illness and, later, cancer. This book is a personal look at Scott's life, the competitive world of skating, his rise to athletic stardom, his creation of *Stars on Ice*, and the knocks he's taken from persistent medical assaults. An inspiring story filled with the infectious spirit of Scott's winning personality.

Kuhlman, Evan, and J. P. Coovert

The Last Invisible Boy

Atheneum Books for Young Readers, 2008   Grades 6–9
Death, trauma, mental illness, recovery

Finn Garrett almost disappears the year "after that terrible thing happened." His hair turns white and his skin gets paler everyday. He writes his story in a journal/comic format that will hold reluctant readers' interest as they unravel the sad year-in-the-life of Finn. While he writes in a simple and lighthearted manner, his underlying sentiments are gentle and poignant. Through the deceptive simplicity, the void in Finn's life—the death of his father—is deeply felt. As Finn's friendship with 12-year-old Melanie becomes more meaningful, he becomes more reflective and braves getting back in touch with the world. A compelling, comical, and compassionate book that will appeal to many readers.

Valens, Evans G.

The Other Side of the Mountain (Part 1)

Warner Books, 1977   Grades 7–12
paralysis, physical disability; biography

The true story of 18-year-old Jill Kinmont, a pretty and gifted 1950s Olympic alpine hopeful. Considered the prettiest girl on the slopes and a rising star to secure an Olympic slot, Jill was featured on the cover of *Sports Illustrated* in January 1955. By the time the magazine hit the stands, Jill was a quadriplegic. A horrible ski accident changed her life in an instant. Through her story, Jill's sights shift from a self-absorbed athlete with huge aspirations to an accident survivor working to move her hands and live a purposeful existence. Her well-balanced disposition is almost uncanny. Jill was a high-spirited teen with refreshing naiveté and typical vanities. How often do you read about accident victims recovering in the clutches of Crutchfield tongs, with tubes in and catheters out, concerned with keeping their body toned and tanned, their lipstick smooth?

Jill's youthful outlook is far-reaching and inspirational. Still later, under a schedule of constant physical therapy, she sets her sights on college. Her family's sacrifice and constant support, her fierce personal determination, the friends who stick by her, the men who don't, and the daredevil guy who caused her great vexation but never allowed her to give up—all contribute to this most captivating story of strength over adversity. Despite happening over 60 years ago, Jill's story remains a gripping page-turner.

Van Draanen, Wendelin
The Running Dream
Alfred A. Knopf, 2011   Grades 8–12
accident, amputation, prosthesis, cerebral palsy

An outstanding runner, 16-year-old Jessica loses her leg in a tragic school bus accident. From waking up in the hospital and coping with the devastating reality to her return home and school, she must resume life and regain a hold on her hopes and dreams—now so seemingly hopeless. On one level the story offers a hand to those dealing with their own misfortunes. It inspires recovery, fight, survival and victory. Supportive family, friends, and community are a huge part of Jessica's success. Ultimately she must reach deep to push past her personal wall of self-pity and loathing, to move ahead with her life. On a deeper level, there is Jessica's blind discrimination against a fellow student, Rosa. Rosa has cerebral palsy; she is hard to understand and easy to ignore. Slowly Jessica and Rosa begin a tentative friendship, and Jessica challenges herself to help Rosa be seen. How Jessica orchestrates putting Rosa into the forefront of the community's consciousness is a study of fierce determination and faith. This story celebrates support, healing, and moving on. Readers will cheer for Jessica's recovery and her awareness of others.

Scrivener, Leslie

Terry Fox: His Story (revised edition)

McClelland and Stewart, 2000 Grades 8–12

cancer, amputation; biography

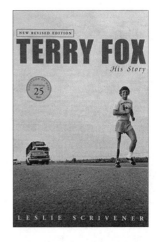

When Terry Fox was diagnosed with osteogenic sarcoma, an aggressive cancer to the bone, he had little time to adjust to the news. In a few short weeks the 18-year-old college athlete was in surgery and his leg was amputated just above the knee. Terry wasted little time on the shocking events; instead, in keeping with the wicked determination that contributed to making him a successful athlete, he set a new goal: once he recovered—and he never doubted that he would—he would run across Canada and raise awareness and money for cancer research. What followed is Terry's story, as riveting as it is painful. His goal was to run a daily marathon—just a bit over twenty-six miles—using his strong leg and a prosthesis constructed of a fiberglass bucket that fit over his stump and a steel shank that extended to the ground. His selfless ambition to raise money was matched only by his excruciating and grueling physical investment. His quest was to keep on running, to broadcast his mission to every small town and large city along the way. He ran 3,318 miles from June through August 1981. When increased medical complications took him off his quest and put him in a hospital, he was still optimistic and motivational. Terry Fox is immortalized in Canada and around the world as an inspirational hero.

Schmidt, Gary D.

Trouble

Clarion Books, 2008 Grades 7–12

accident, abuse, depression, class conflict, ethnic prejudice

When Henry's brother, Franklin, a star high school athlete, is hit by a car, the invincibility of their family household takes a blow. They are a family of lineage with a long-standing blue-blood reputation. They live in a huge family home overlooking the ocean; trouble is not to touch them. The high school driver of the car, Chay, is a young Cambodian immigrant. He is charged with a hit-and-run. He tells the judge he fell asleep at the wheel, that he stayed by Franklin's side trying to stem the blood pouring from Franklin's severed arm, and then ran for help. Nonetheless the community sees the accident as a Cambodian enemy assault on Franklin. Complicating things further is Chay's clandestine romance with Henry and Franklin's teen sister.

Chay takes on the sickening responsibility for the accident. Henry is tormented by the accident as well as memories of big brother Franklin: his all-school popularity, notable athletic feats, but also his underlying abusive mean streak that Henry knows too well. In an ironic twist of fate Chay and Henry are thrown together for a wilderness adventure journey fraught with extreme emotional and physical challenges.

As in life, little is as it seems in this story. There are layers of misunderstanding and missteps in family relationships and terrible inequities in social and cultural justice. This page-turner, while serious in subject matter, is lightened by humorous boy dialogue and infused with the healing spirit of willpower and good intentions.

Smith, Doris Buchanan
Voyages: A Novel
Viking, 1989   Grades 6–9
assault, physical trauma, psychological trauma, recovery

Twelve-year-old Janessa is recovering from a violent attack after she was abducted from a store, beaten up, and thrown out of a speeding car. Now in a hospital bed, her head clutched in a vise known as Crutchfield tongs, her leg pinned down by weights and pulleys, she is safe but hurting and haunted by vicious memories. Emotionally and physically traumatized, Janessa pulls away from her daily reality by escaping to a land of Norse mythological adventure. Janessa's narrative hesitantly steps beyond the confines of her body, the terror of her memories, and the hours of boredom lying nearly paralyzed while awaiting visits from her parents, a teacher, nurses, or the doctors. She enters a time-switch alternative universe, escaping the bed and teleporting to an imaginary land. The healing power of mythological escape and the metaphorical explanation that Janessa slowly accepts allow her to tentatively return and face her life. As difficult as Janessa's experience and the work she has ahead of her are, there is a tremendous amount of love and support from her surrounding family members. This is a gentle tale told through the narrative of the victim, mapping her imaginative escape to a safe harbor as she steers her way back to recovery.

NOTES

1. Leslie Scrivener, *Terry Fox: His Story* (Toronto: McClelland and Stewart, 1981), 24, 33.

2. Laurie Lawlor, *Helen Keller: Rebellious Spirit* (New York: Holiday House, 2001), 65.

3. Barbara Chai, "How Brian Selznick Got the Inspiration for 'Wonderstruck,'" *Speakeasy, Wall Street Journal*, September 13, 2011, http://blogs.wsj.com/speakeasy/2011/09/13/how-brian -selznick-got-the-inspiration-for-wonderstruck.

Stories of Disorders and Differences

Autism, Asperger's, and Tourette's

There are more and more titles available that feature young characters afflicted with one of any number of mental disorders. At the risk of sounding glib, at the time of this writing, autism is popular because the disorder is receiving much attention in popular culture, including contemporary young adult and children's literature. Many of the stories are realistic, personal portrayals; some are written by authors who have an autistic child, and others are by authors who have practiced as mental health counselors or are involved in the mental health field. Several are personal memoirs. Cory Friedman's story, coauthored by James Patterson and Cory's father, Hal Friedman, is about a young boy driven to the brink of insanity by an onslaught of spasmodic interruptions from Tourette's syndrome. With Cory's consent, Hal Friedman felt compelled to share how 13 difficult years of contending with Tourette's destroyed Cory's childhood and adolescence. When Hal asked Cory about publicizing his story, Cory responded, "If it will help people like me, yes."[1]

Author Suzanne Crowley's daughter was diagnosed with Asperger's syndrome. When Crowley wrote her novel *The Very Ordered Existence of Marilee Marvelous,* she thought she'd be the first person to have an autistic main character, but by then *The Curious Incident of the Dog in the Night-Time* had been published. In her article "The Voices of Autism," Crowley writes of becoming curious about what others had written: "What I found were some richly textured works with highly unusual voices, individuals trying to cope and navigate their worlds in unusual ways, and, most surprisingly, characters who possessed sharp insights into human nature and who had much to teach us. . . . To simply dismiss adolescent literature with autism as the current hot thing greatly misses the mark. There is much in these works that will resonate with all readers, whether they have a disability or not. The trials and triumphs of the human heart are the same for all." Blaze Ginsberg (*Episodes: My Life As I See It*) says, "I try to connect with the world like everyone else, through people, my family and friends." Adds Cynthia Lord (*Rules*), "I keep one e-mail from a 10-year-old sibling on the wall next to my desk. It says simply, 'I was so scared I was the only person who felt this way.' Sometimes books say the things we can't."[2]

The autism spectrum is vast, from children who are completely and irreversibly withdrawn into their own world, to high-functioning kids who sometimes behave oddly but often perform brilliantly. Autism is mysterious and can be heartbreaking. Some individuals are content within their own worlds, while others seem tormented and trapped. An autistic child may live within a bell jar, and the responsibility falls to those in the "normal" world to reach and support the child. It is perplexing and mystifying and can be daunting. While there are distinct symptoms that seem to fit across the board and affect all autistic children, not all children will display all the symptoms.

Writers communicate the distinct and subtle personalities of their characters through tone, reflective narrative, and conversational dialogue. When a reader travels with the character, instead of perceiving a flat character labeled with a pitiful disorder, the reader knows what it's like to be unencumbered by social manners, obligations, or influences—what it feels like to have sounds and touch amplified to the point of excruciating intensity. Maybe the reader empathizes with the heightened sensitivity, or even envies some characters for their acute concentration, their indifference toward outside opinion, and their intelligent affinity for specific interests. Or perhaps the reader feels compassionate toward the suffering. Ultimately, readers accept and respect differences.

Pulitzer Prize–winning author Tim Page was diagnosed with Asperger's syndrome as an adult. He writes,

> In the years since the phrase became a cliché, I have received any number of compliments for my supposed ability to "think outside the box." Actually, it has been a struggle for me to perceive just what these "boxes" were—why they were there, why other people regarded them as important, where their borderlines might be, how to live safely within and without them. My efforts have been only partly successful: after fifty-two years, I am left with the melancholy sensation that my life has been spent in a perpetual state of parallel play, alongside, but distinctly apart from, the rest of humanity.[3]

Or consider Francisco Stork's 17-year-old Marcelo, from the book *Marcelo in the Real World*. Diagnosed with Asperger's syndrome, Marcelo has attended Paterson, a school for special needs students. His father, Arturo, wants Marcelo in the mainstream of "the real world." He'll work in Arturo's law office—starting in the mail room—over the summer. Marcelo considers:

> I am thinking that next fall, I will be able to work full-time at Paterson training Fritzy and the other ponies. I can visit the ponies on the weekends this summer. Arturo is basically asking me to pretend that I am normal, according to his definition, for three months. This is an impossible task, as far as I can tell, especially since it is very difficult for me to feel that I am not normal. Why can't others think and see the world the way I see it? But after three months, it will be over, and I can be who I am.

Marcelo submits to his father's dream. In the mail room a coworker asks:

> "I meant, what's wrong with you, with the way you think? Your father said you had some kind of cognitive disorder."
>
> "He said that?" It surprises me to hear Arturo refer to me that way. He has always insisted that there's nothing wrong with me. The term "cognitive disorder" implies that there is something wrong with the way I think or with the way I perceive reality. I perceive reality just fine. Sometimes I perceive more of reality than others.

A bit later Marcelo continues to reflect upon the question:

> This is a topic of conversation that I am knowledgeable about but not particularly fond of. Explanations about my condition are based on the assumption that there is something wrong with the way I am, and at Paterson I have learned through the years that it is not helpful to view myself or the other kids there that way. I view myself as different in the way I think, talk, and act, but not as someone who is abnormal or ill. But how do I explain the differences to people?[4]

Such passages contained within a plot of intrigue, corruption, and romance can nudge attention away from oneself and inspire consideration of the fascinating differences of others. Those readers diagnosed with a disorder may feel a connection and comfort knowing that they are not alone in their intense focus, patterns, and social discomforts. Instead of general misunderstanding and a sense of discord, readers are empowered by their individuality.

Marc Nobleman's nonfiction graphic novel *Boys of Steel: The Creators of Superman* has had interesting reactions. While the book never suggests that writer Jerry Siegel or artist Joe Shuster (the creators of *Superman*) have a disorder, the description of their teen behaviors say otherwise. Here's a response from Marc Nobleman's blog from the mother of two boys—one in elementary school, the other in middle school:

> Both of my boys have Asperger's [syndrome]. They both are highly intelligent. The combination of high IQ and Asperger's makes their lives more complicated. It is a challenge for them to fit in socially and to relate to other people. What makes it worse is that they know they don't fit in.
>
> When [my older son] read *Boys of Steel,* his first comment was that he was very much like the boys who created Superman. He was very excited that this was a true story. It meant that there were other people like him. He even made a list of the ways he was similar to Jerry and Joe (quiet, wears glasses, doesn't fit in, likes to write, and likes to draw). He then read the author's note at the back of the book. He was not happy about how their lives turned out. He said it was a lesson for him to try harder to overcome his anxieties and try new things.
>
> My younger son also read the book later. He also related to the characters. He said that they were just like him. He had not heard my conversation with my older son. He said that now when he gets pushed around he is going to remember Jerry and Joe and how they made Superman![5]

I have watched a child with high-functioning Asperger's syndrome stand up at her graduation and give thanks and display emotional gratitude. She giggled self-consciously, kept her eyes averted from the crowd, and spoke haltingly as she proudly stated, "I am not the same girl who came here three years ago." She had friends. She had a roommate. She went on trips with other students. She read books, and she wrote about how they affected her. She told me, "I liked *Marcelo in the Real World.* He reminded me of myself. Well, not me, but of my brother. My brother is very smart but he goes to a special school and most people don't understand him." The truth is, Marcelo is very much like her: disarmingly honest, unabashedly intelligent, naive in the face of manipulative behavior, having an intuitive connection with animals and dismayed by social graces. Sometimes I would say good morning and she would walk right past me, silently absorbed in her own thoughts. Yet like Marcelo, she is figuring out how to act "normal," fit in, and live in the real world. Of significant relevance is her identity and connection to a fictionalized character that validates her own, and her family's, differences.

In Nora Raleigh Baskin's *Anything but Typical,* Jason, the 12-year-old main character, writes, "Neurotypicals like it when you look them in the eye. It is supposed to mean you are listening, as if the reverse were true, which it is not: just because you are not looking at someone does not mean you are not listening. I can listen better when I am not distracted by the person's face: What are their eyes saying? Is that a frown or a smile? Why are they wrinkling their forehead or lifting their cheeks like that? What does that mean?" And later on he reflects,

> How do you show appreciation? Appreciation is an emotion. It's a feeling. You can't draw a picture of it. Why do people want everyone to act just like they do?
> Talk like they do. Look like they do. Act like they do.
> And if you don't—
> If you don't, people make the assumption that you do not feel what they feel.
> And then they make the assumption—
> That you must not feel anything at all[6]

While the plot and setting are fictitious, Suzanne Crowley explains that many of the characteristics for her character Merilee are based on her daughter:

> My daughter notices other things that the rest of our family doesn't. Asperger's children often seem like they are somewhere else, that they're not paying attention. They are really observing and they often notice things that no one else does. She will pick up on the undercurrent of a conversation and make sly comments that clue us in that she's listening. When they were younger her sister would become frustrated with her and snip, "Stop talking like an old lady." She used odd phrases and had an advanced vocabulary. While I was writing *Merilee,* editors were saying, "She doesn't sound autistic enough."
>
> My daughter didn't want to read *The Very Ordered Existence of Merilee Marvelous* until it was out in hardback. Everyone else was reading it, librarians, reviewers, but she hadn't read it. I was receiving responses from life skills and special education teachers who "got it." I also heard from families who recognized their own kids. So one day I came home and said to her, "You really need to read this." She went up to her room and came down about an hour

later. She said "It's really eerie how you have me nailed. You have all my inner thoughts." Now that the book has been out for awhile I receive e-mails from readers who write, "I'm just like Merilee, quiet with no friends."[7]

Stories about children with special needs unveil their particular and seemingly peculiar world. In daily life their peer group may ignore them. Walking with an autistic character within the confines of a story, for example, can give one an experience of visiting a house of mirrors—the reader's equilibrium shifts to navigate with the character through what is no longer a static, known, and balanced perception. What was clear becomes abstract and vice versa.

These stories also help the reader contemplate the age-old question of what *normal* really is. One of my students responded to *The Reinvention of Edison Thomas,* "I liked how Eddy reacted to surprises and how the author made Eddy seem like a real person. Sometimes he reminded me of myself. I felt like if I went to his school I would be able to find him jumping on the trampoline, or talking to his counselor, Tiffany, or smashing ketchup packets in the cafeteria. This was about Eddy finding who he is and who his real friends are."

Finally, what about children and teens diagnosed with a disorder? What do they like to read? Suzanne Crowley's daughter, now a college student and aspiring writer, responded,

> The Redwall books [by Brian Jacques] were what got me into reading. I remember that one of my favorite books in the series was *Outcast of Redwall* because the story featured a weasel who was raised to be good at the Redwall monastery. Weasels are always evil in the series, so I really hoped that Veil, the weasel, would grow up to be good, but there were many conflicts in the story that pushed him to be evil in the end. So that made it a sad story for me definitely, and I still often like those "in-between" characters.

She comprehends the complexities of character development, the very real conflicts in life, and accepts the unhappy resolution.

> I also started reading Harry Potter when I was eleven, the same age as Harry is in the first book . . . I remember reading other fantasy books like *A Wrinkle in Time* [by Madeleine L'Engle], *Abarat* [by Clive Barker], and His Dark Materials trilogy [by Philip Pullman]. For these books, I think the strangeness of the different creatures and worlds really set off my imagination.

I liked a lot of fantasy when I was little but I think the stranger the worlds were, the more I wanted them to be real.

A sensitive child with a vivid imagination, astute awareness, and creative vision discovers that a world where everyone conforms to the standard is a bit dull and disappointing.

A library branch manager from the New Orleans area is the mother of two children diagnosed with Asperger's disorder. She shared her findings on what autistic children liked to read. She's served as a teacher for eight years and a youth services librarian for two years, and she speaks from knowledge and experience and was very clear that these children do not like reading anything that is mean, upsetting, or had to do with bullying. She says,

> game guides (while this sounds silly, the guides are very in depth and require a lot of reading), Pokémon graphic novels and guides (called a Pokedex), Magic Tree House series, Mo Willems's books (*Don't Let the Pigeon Drive the Bus!*), and Tedd Arnold's Fly Guy series . . . I find that these books can be put in categories: graphic novels, books about things they like (Legos, Star Wars, Pokémon, video games, animals, World War II, etc.), informational books with facts and graphics, funny books, visually pleasing books, and books they choose—rather than books that are assigned—when they have to read a chapter book for school.
>
> They shy away from any books where there is a lot of bullying in them ([one boy] quit *Diary of a Wimpy Kid* because of it) or books that are really thick in size (they are intimidating). They tend to shy away from sad stories or stories with stressful situations. For the most part, kids that I have encountered are looking for fiction books that are escapes (usually humorous) or very factual books (they may deal with hard topics like the holocaust but they don't delve into the emotional side of it). The older one had to read *Number the Stars* and he was sad for weeks afterward.
>
> As far as special needs characters, I find that the kids that I have encountered like books where they can identify with the main character but not when the character's "difference" is pointed out . . . I do think that stories with special needs protagonists are important especially for the "non-special needs" crowd. I find that the Asperger's crowd does not trend towards realistic fiction. This is because books that tell a story that could happen to them can cause anxiety, especially if the story deals with bullying.

My must-reads books right now are: Percy Jackson and the Olympians series and the Harry Potter series—Percy has dyslexia and Harry has more of an overall "not fitting in" problem. In both of these, the character's "special needs" is not the point of the story. Kids can relate to these characters as being different.[8]

The following stories are not about disorders but about people finding their way in a challenging world. What may appear to be strange people in strange predicaments are real people who wake up every day to face their fears: make friends, find solutions, reach their potential, live in harmony with their family members, and push beyond their different perspectives. As we all do.

Suggested Reading

Baskin, Nora Raleigh
Anything but Typical
Simon & Schuster Books for Young Readers, 2009   Grades 5–9
autism

Jason spends lots of energy trying to control his flapping hands and ignore the many irritants that cause him frequent discomfort: the cold grass, too much noise, bright lights. He's progressed to the mainstream classroom, a step that brings his mother relief and Jason grief. He's alienated within this class, not included in conversations, and certainly not invited to parties. The kids are mean and shun him. Jason searches elsewhere for a community and finds it on the Internet. He discovers an online website called Storyboard. As a contributing member of this virtual writers group, he has success telling his stories and displaying his feelings, and he begins to develop a sense of self-worth and identity. Through the online creative forum Jason meets Rebecca and dreams of romance. When he lands a trip to the Storyboard conference in Texas, what are the chances that he'll meet up with her? Will he discover the things that are really important to him at the conference? This story includes a realistic progression of overcoming obstacles and growing through reflection.

Nobleman, Marc Tyler, and Ross MacDonald
Boys of Steel:
The Creators of Superman
A. A. Knopf, 2008   Grades 4–12
depression, shyness, Asperger's syndrome; nonfiction

On the surface, the man of steel does not carry the stuff of learning disabilities, dysfunctions, or disorders. He is so above it all! The truth is, Superman's creators were two shy and quiet teens who found it painful and disheartening to walk through the halls of high school. The boys, Jerry Siegel and Joe Shuster, outcasts at school, spent hours designing their ultra alter ego at home. They invested their dreams and aspirations creating a secret identity that successfully hit the pulp comic world.

Jerry was introspective and haunted by the untimely death of his father. He escaped into the lives of comic book heroes—*Flash Gordon, Tarzan and Buck Rogers*—the exciting action figures of the time, and created his own excitement through writing. Joe was a loner with a similar insecure temperament. He escaped his uncomfortable high school years by drawing. Like Jerry, he enjoyed the fictionalized world of archetypical heroes.

The two teens collaborated their talents, creating a superhero who rose above the disappointment of their daily planet. Superman was the embodiment of all that they were not: strong, confident, courageous, athletic, empowered, handsome, and best of all, worshiped by the girls. He was the ironic double-faced fantasy of everyman. His lackluster appearance as Clark Kent was a cover-up. He was on alert, hunting down and tackling evil forces that lurked on every street—from Metropolis to Smallville—and winning girls' hearts.

This graphic nonfiction story, set against the Great Depression of the 1930s and leading up to the United States' entry into World War II, tells the fascinating story of how two oddball teenagers developed a super-secret identity born from their imaginations. Jerry and Joe were each just 24 years old when they launched their brainchild. *Superman* became an instant and unprecedented success, though the two fought a lifelong battle for recognition and royalties. Their story is certain to capture the imaginations of children who think differently and dare to leap tall dreams.

~~~~~~

Billingsley, Franny

Chime

Dial Books, 2011   Grades 7–12

guilt, self-blame, repetitive behavior, mental disability

Seventeen-year-old Briony is haunted by the guilt of her stepmother's death— a stepmother who whispered evil spells and insinuations, convincing Briony of her dark

Additional Titles of Interest Featured in Other Chapters

Athletic Shorts: Six Short Stories (chapter 3, page 21)

Big Nate: In a Class by Himself (chapter 3, page 22)

The Crazy Horse Electric Game (chapter 5, page 75)

Notes from the Dog (chapter 5, page 69).

Rules (chapter 3, page 32)

What Are You Afraid Of? Stories about Phobias (chapter 4, page 45)

intent and a marred future. Briony harbors self-loathing for her consuming secret. Twin sister Rose has a mental disorder that Briony is certain she has caused. Rose gets stuck on things; she cannot bear to hear the Mirk and the Midnight Hour chimes; she must wear only certain colored ribbons; she knows that it's exactly 564 steps to the firehouse; she slows time by shutting herself in a wardrobe; and she prefers not to wear shoes. Briony cares for Rose with the assumed dogmatic right of being her twin sister. She tries to coax Rose beyond her odd habits through reason and compromise. Now Rose has contracted the ominous swamp cough, a cough that claims too many lives. Briony is steadfast in her mission to save her twin's life.

Accompanying the village swirl of witch hunts and hangings, the tension mounts when a railroad magnate plans to drain the Swampsea. By setting progress into motion, he unleashes dire reactions from the spirit world. The handsome Eldric, son of the developer, enters the scene with his quick wit and tender spirit. Briony is subsequently charmed and cursed with the task of maintaining balance of her twinship, of her mystical powers, and of superstitious village lore.

Part gothic romance, part exotic enchantment tale, this is also a twin balance of characters: courageous Briony, witchy wolf-girl, and curious Rose, structured and painstakingly rigid in her rituals. (Briony is a wryly humorous narrator, but frequently it is Rose who steals the show.) A story based in folklore and imagination, tethered to the realistic patterns of psychological trauma, conflict, and resolution. Irresistible.

Haddon, Mark
The Curious Incident of the Dog in the Night-Time
Doubleday, 2003   Grades 7–12
Asperger's syndrome

In this mystery Christopher is accused of murdering the neighbor's dog. In fact, he is distraught over the senselessness of the murder but unable to articulate his unease. Christopher is mathematically gifted and socially inept. He is unable to understand the social cues around him, the unsettling behaviors of his parents, or the mystifying mistrust of strangers. With an emotionless intent, Christopher is compelled to piece the incidents of the dog's murder together and determined to solve the mystery. Perhaps one of the strongest elements of this story is how dry and unaffected it is. It unfolds with a droll British tone that is intensified by Christopher's powers of observation; he is keenly astute, forgetting nothing and piecing clues together with Sherlock mastery, yet he behaves oddly and seems emotionally wrung out, and removed from the action.

Christopher is encouraged by his school counselor to write a book about his investigations. The result, told in a factually heavy but detached voice, comes complete with illustrations and prime-numbered chapters.

Ginsberg, Blaze

Episodes: My Life as I See It

Roaring Brook Press, 2009   Grades 8–12

autism; memoir

In an unusual format that unfolds like the panning of a video camera—complete with camera shots, tangential trivia descriptions, cast lists, dialogue, and director's notes—Blaze reveals his thought process and personality. This is a memoir of a 17-year-old who is diagnosed with high-functioning autism, attends a very supportive special school, and is able to compartmentalize sequences of his life as though they're episodes on TV. Creatively, he shows his perspective, often as a peripheral observer, yet simultaneously he appears as a cast member. This is one interesting book, with a loose and wobbling plot, that explains the day-to-day experience of navigating through the world in a very singular way.

Hesser, Terry Spencer

Kissing Doorknobs

Delacorte Press, 1998   Grades 5–12

obsessive-compulsive disorder, mental illness

Tara is clutched in a vise of irrational repetitive thoughts and embarrassing behaviors. In kindergarten, she has disproportionate fears: constant, unrelenting concern for her parents' safety; a routine school fire drill; recurring nightmares; her closet door left open—all send her into panic. Her family and teachers consider her high-strung. In an instant, the overly sensitive, seemingly normal 11-year-old Tara, "still in possession" of her own thoughts, experiences a metaphorical mental crack that she's unable to silence or ignore for the next 4 years. Tara knows that to speak about her fears is to invite ridicule, shame, and disbelief. She strives to keep her obsessive thoughts and actions secret, not wanting to risk the admission that she may be going insane. As Tara's quirks and odd behaviors intensify, so do the reaction and response from her family—a protective sister, a melodramatic mother, and a father in denial. Her friends call her "odd" but love her for her wit, honesty, and differences. Feeling the dreadful nag of obsessive thoughts, the reader follows Tara's hopeless sense of despair. Tara is lonely, powerless to break free from the incessant chattering in her head. Readers also feel the pain, exasperation, and finally, the resentment from her loving family members. For all of Tara's emotional intensity, the reader is sustained by her spirit and humor: she is funny, even while she suffers. Don't let the cover or the title fool you—this one's not to be missed.

~~~~~~

Stork, Francisco X.

Marcelo in the Real World

Arthur A. Levine Books, 2009   Grades 8–12
Asperger's syndrome, depression

For 17-year-old Marcelo, living with Asperger's syndrome is not a problem—it's who he is. Self-absorbed privacy is his comfort zone. Marcelo listens to his pleasant internal music and sleeps in a tree house in his parents' backyard. He attends a school for special needs students, where he is comfortable, content, and successful working with the therapy ponies. His father, Arturo, a high-powered lawyer, demands that Marcelo learn to live in "the real world." He assigns Marcelo work in his law office—starting in the mail room—for the summer, gambling on the unrealistic notion that Marcelo will adjust, change, and want to be mainstreamed in his high school senior year. Marcelo is clearly disappointed not to be able to spend his summer working with the ponies. Obedient and characteristically black-and-white, Marcelo is willing to test his father's dream for the summer.

Arturo's office is blessed with the gem of Jasmine, Marcelo's mail room boss. Otherwise, the law firm is dominated by colleagues with unethical intentions (including Wendell, the cocky young son of his father's partner). Marcelo, unable to decipher facial expression or unravel untoward verbal connotations, is already at an extreme social disadvantage. He innocently trusts people with questionable motives and is plunged into a confusing, conflicting, but ultimately awakening summer. This is a story that teens love. Marcelo's flat assessment is authentic, his perspective revealing, the action fast, and the underlying romance delightful.

Patterson, James, and Hal Friedman

Med Head: My Knock-Down, Drag-Out, Drugged-Up Battle with My Brain

Little, Brown and Company, 2010   Grades 7–12

Tourette's syndrome, obsessive-compulsive disorder, anxiety; nonfiction

Cory Friedman was a normal healthy 5-year-old boy—and then, he wasn't. This tells the true story of how Cory was suddenly and inexplicably afflicted with uncontrollable physical spasms and tics caused by Tourette's syndrome. He spirals down fast into a mysterious quagmire of messed up body wiring that sends mega surges of energy to unprepared body zones. One day he's fine; the next he's physically shocked by muscle spasms and uncontrollable reflexes so intense that they break his teeth and crack his ribs. No less extreme are the facial tics, spitting, strange noises, and parroting. He's haunted by horrible thoughts, panicked by irrational fears, and severely anxious and overwrought by contending with it all. What complicates Cory's already awful predicament is that medical doctors know little about his condition and even less about how to treat him. Despite the tireless advocacy of his family, he spends 13 years like a tormented guinea pig, cycling through medicines that do little to help and often worsen his symptoms. Thirteen doctors, 60 potent pharmaceutical prescriptions and a 50-pound weight gain from the side effects of his medication, do nothing to alleviate his debilitating symptoms. The only positive outlet is from physical activity; he's an athletic team star and successfully completes a therapeutic wilderness program. Unfortunately, the very real benefits of physical activity aren't seriously considered as a potential remedy. Into his adolescence, with few friends, he follows a frustrating trail of ineffective medical treatment. His physical torment is ratcheted up with high anxiety and depression, which Cory attempts to self-medicate with alcohol. With the support of his parents, the assistance of a persistent doctor, and Cory's own determined fortitude, eventually there's a marked turnaround and finally, slow relief and progress. There is also the fact that for no apparent reason, when Cory is about 18 years old, his Tourette's syndrome seems to regress, allowing him to lead a more independent life. This is an inspirational stranger-than-fiction survival tale.

Erskine, Kathryn
Mockingbird (Mok'ing-bûrd)
Philomel Books, 2010   Grades 5–7
Asperger's syndrome, trauma, death

As the title suggests, this story has a metaphoric connection to the novel *To Kill a Mockingbird*. Ten-year-old Caitlin has Asperger's syndrome. Her mother died of cancer three years before, and her father is suspended in the trauma that began "The Day Our Life Fell Apart"—when Devon, her older brother, is killed in a school shooting. This leaves Caitlin and her father alone together, struggling to cope.

Caitlin is an artist with a gifted talent that far exceeds her age; she has already won a major art competition. She confines herself to creating black-and-white images, reflective of how she sees the world—a perspective she won't budge from. While her Asperger's dictates her puzzling, tightly wired behavior, it's her sensitive school guidance counselor who slowly draws her toward closure about Devon. The story also ties in to *To Kill a Mockingbird*, especially connecting Caitlin to the character Scout. With her counselor's steadfast help and using Harper Lee's classic as a frame, Caitlin is made aware of the value of friendship, her father's pain, and her own unbearable loss, and confronts the sickening "recess" in her stomach as she's pushed beyond her denial to experience empathy.

~~~~~~~~~~~~~~~~~~~~~~~~~~~~~~~~~~~~~~~

Gallo, Donald, ed.
Owning It: Stories about Teens with Disabilities
Candlewick Press, 2008   Grades 7–12
physical, psychological, and medical challenges

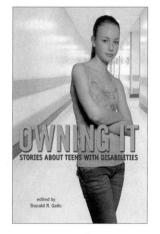

This anthology introduces teens with a mix of physical, psychological, and medical problems. From asthma to Tourette's, from addiction to ADHD, the disorders and settings are both broad and diverse. Robert Lipsyte's story about cancer and chemo is a creative and compassionate survival tale. Recuperating in the hospital, several boys share one commonality, the unnerving wait for their prognoses. With varying degrees of success they accept their sentence. At the heart of this tale is the group support they summon against their individual helplessness; a flawless short story about an otherwise unimaginable experience. Chris Crutcher, a staunch advocate for the mistreated and misunderstood, portrays the frustrations of an intelligent boy with ADD trapped in the classroom. Eddie, with his racing and obsessive thoughts, suffers the interminable classroom clock and fails to wrestle his quick-witted defensive diatribe into submission. David Lubar's "Here's to Good Friends" tells the story of Brad, the surviving drunk driver in an accident that allegedly kills two friends. In "Tic and Shout" we meet Alex, who is trying to manage his Tourette's syndrome and flow into the mainstream. When you're different and uncontrollably disruptive, middle school culture is ugly. Kids call him Dog Boy and Mad Dog. He is determined to break free from the protective confines of homeschooling. He describes his fits of barking, swearing, noise-making, and tics: "It's like someone opened my head and stirred with a stick." When Alex courageously and uninhibitedly attends the school dance, there is both a show of success and a response of kindness. In another story, a girl lives in terror of the lurking onset of chronic and extreme migraines that take her out for days, while an accident victim juggles the teen social scene from her wheelchair. Some characters hang on to hope; others strive to accept an unfortunate twist of fate, but all the stories here provide awareness to prevalent and debilitating situations that are too often ignored.

Page, Tim

Parallel Play: Growing up with Undiagnosed Asperger's

Doubleday, 2009   Grade 9–adult

Asperger's syndrome; memoir

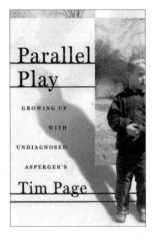

In this autobiographical account, Pulitzer Prize winner Tim Page describes the confusion, perplexity, and depression caused by living with undiagnosed Asperger's syndrome for 45 years. While Page was always considered bright—often called a genius—he was also odd and incapable of fitting in. This left him lonely with prevalent feelings of alienation. He writes,

> I was forty-five years old when I learned that I wasn't alone . . . I've spent too much of my life isolated, unhappy, and conflicted—yet I am also convinced that many of the things I've done were accomplished not despite my Asperger's syndrome but *because* of it. I'm sure that it's responsible, at least in part, for my powers of concentration, which permit me to absorb a congenial subject

immediately, write an article in an afternoon or a book in a summer, blotting out everyone and everything until the project is completed . . .

Nevertheless, my strangeness persists and I know that there is a lot that simply slips by. I can have lunch with somebody and come away with no memory of what she was wearing. I still neglect my shirttails, my shoelaces, and, on rare and embarrassing occasions, my zipper. If someone were to ask me to close my eyes right now and describe the clothes I had on today, I would have to think hard about it and might well answer incorrectly. (pp. 178–179)

Tim Page is a clear and precise thinker and an articulate writer, and his story leads the reader smack into a world of a creative visionary with immeasurable intelligence and keen awareness.

~~~~~~

Houtman, Jacqueline

The Reinvention of Edison Thomas

Front Street, 2010   Grades 7–9
Asperger's syndrome

Eddy is determined to win the school's science fair competition and is distraught when he doesn't. When the disappointment coupled with the noise level in the gymnasium peaks, he curls up on the floor, covers his ears, rocks his body, and chants chemical compounds to himself. Eddy's sensitive nerves are like antennae sweeping the air, picking up anxieties that cause him to recoil. Eddy has high-functioning Asperger's syndrome. His intolerance of other students' experiments, their limitations, and their noise level is real—as real as the people who avoid Eddy and his odd behaviors. Old playmates grow up and become mean adolescents. Eddy overlooks the students who try to befriend him because he is unable to understand their social cues. Nothing is simple for Eddy, and when the school's crossing guard is let go, Eddy obsesses over every imaginable calamity that could happen to children heedless of cars that may fail to stop. Following his counselor's advice, he puts his worry to work. He spends hours in his basement inventing a traffic signal device. He loves the structure of science and tinkers endlessly with recycled gizmos and wires.

This is a curious walk with a mind that's fine-tuned to many different frequencies. Inserting Latin scientific names and a bank of "random access memory" of scientific trivia (correlating to numeric figures) underscores Eddy's extreme intelligence and fierce concentration.

Angleberger, Tom, and Jason L. Rosenstock

The Strange Case of Origami Yoda

Amulet Books, 2010   Grades 4–7
Asperger's syndrome, bullying

The superhero in this graphic novel is Origami Yoda, a finger puppet who sits on dweeby Dwight's finger and offers sage advice to sixth-grade kids who spend more time laughing at Dwight than with him. But wait a minute—they are taking Origami Yoda seriously! The story is also about friends, bullies, a guy, a girl, and kids stuffed into the confines of sixth grade.

Told in journal format, Tommy, the main narrator, threads the story together. The looming question: is Origami Yoda real? In Tommy's words, "The strange thing about Origami Yoda is that he is so wise even though Dwight is a total loser. I'm not saying that as an insult. It's just a fact. Dwight never seems to do anything right. Always in trouble. Always getting harassed by other kids. Always picking his nose. Always finding a way to 'ruin it for everyone,' as the teachers say" (pp. 3–4).

The saving grace is that through Origami Yoda, Dwight unwittingly discovers his power. Origami Yoda, his alter ego, shows the flip side of his clueless behavior—the power of a personality that won't fit in a box or be crumpled by the crowd. Dwight is a keen observer of the social quagmire that rages around him. While seemingly immersed in his own imaginative world of quirkiness, he shoots laser beams of common sense toward those who pay attention.

A choice book to prompt conversation—is it OK to be different? Is Dwight asking for trouble? On the surface this is one silly graphic novel with a bunch of dueling sixth-grade voices, but if you're interested in going to the next level, this is definitely a force to reckon with.

Crowley, Suzanne Carlisle

The Very Ordered Existence of Merilee Marvelous

Greenwillow Books, 2007   Grades 6–9
Asperger's syndrome, fetal alcohol syndrome

Merilee, at 13 and a half, is organized and structured to a fault. The cogs in her well-oiled wheel are living in the eccentric podunk town of Jumbo, Texas, and anything else that messes with her routine—which, on any given day, is everything. This puts Merilee in a very disgruntled, out-of-sorts mood. Merilee has Asperger's syndrome, and while she becomes agitated and bristly, she may become the most engaging, endearing, and enthralling character with a character disorder that you'll have the pleasure to meet. She is filled with matter-of-fact, no-nonsense assessments of the world that surrounds her and the pitfalls that challenge her: "There's a thin line between genius and bottom-barrel stupidness. I hover delicately on a tightrope between the two, wondering where I'll land if I ever fall" (p. 3).

As siblings will, her sister taunts her mercilessly. More surprisingly, her cantankerous grandmother berates her like a mean old cur. Her mom supports and celebrates Merilee's special characteristics. Then Merilee meets 8-year-old Biswick, a boy brain-damaged by fetal alcohol syndrome who trails Merilee like a lovesick puppy; a very disorderly turn of events begins. Biswick carries on an incessant, good-humored chatter and goads Merilee out of her precise preoccupations, pulls her away from the vortex of her inner pools, and introduces her to the marvelous, murky quandary of life's imperfections.

The story is brimming with well-developed characters—flawed and fabulous—in a quirky Texas town, and traveling along in the very ordered existence of Merilee is a marvelous and memorable experience.

Brenna, Beverley A.

Waiting for No One

Red Deer Press, 2010　　　　　　　　Grades 9–12
Asperger's syndrome

In the sequel to *Wild Orchid* (p. 102), 19-year-old Taylor Jane is back home, applying for a bookstore position. Taylor wants to master her fear of not being employable or able to live independently. She's stuck with the bitter irony of feeling alone yet ever dependent. Getting her résumé ready, she prints it out on blue paper ("a more advanced form of white" [p. 4]), lists her pet gerbil as a reference, and includes Asperger's as one of her seven strengths. Taylor's personal narrative sketches out her carefully planned and uncomfortably navigated world. She struggles to understand—and not flip out—over figurative language. Waiting to hear back about the job, she's terrified by the probable answer and arms her days with charms, her favorite numbers, and her favorite colors. She battles swear words that bubble out unbidden during nervousness; she copes with anxiety swaddled under obsessive behaviors.

Her dad has a new life, but Taylor remains his beloved, if challenging, daughter. A turning point comes after Taylor panics destructively over her missing gerbil, forcing her to face the internal mayhem that afflicts her. Taylor's powers of observation are keen, and her story is bemusing and beguiling. Her earnestness, her honesty, her desire to be independent, and her unyielding determination to face her fears will appeal to everyone.

Wild Orchid

Red Deer Press, 2005   Grades 7–12
Asperger's syndrome

Eighteen-year-old Taylor Jane is being dragged against her will to the summer resort of Saskatchewan's Prince Albert National Park. She's following her mom, who is following yet another boyfriend to work in his pizza restaurant for the summer. Taylor Jane has Asperger's syndrome and does not like change. Situations that she can't predict or control make her twitchy. She needs routine and doesn't like the greasy-haired, nine-words-to-a-sentence man her mother has hooked up with. Once in the park, Taylor tries to face some of her fears, taking walks on the beach alone and investigating the nature center. In a lucky twist of fate, she is offered a job at the bookstore there. For Taylor Jane, these small steps of independence and her employment success are tremendous achievements. Along with facing situations that make her uncomfortable, she's pursuing the potential of a "boyfriend," but without the ability to read faces, emotions, or intent, her success is disappointing. Interestingly, Taylor's boyfriend search—and disappointment—aren't that different from most teens; there's more allure to the idea than to the reality. The questionable attentions, the center's director, suggest an underlying intent that's discomfiting. While the reader picks up on his inappropriate interest, characteristically, Taylor does not.

Taylor Jane's voice is not merely candid and easy to follow; her narrative is also easy to identify with and humorous. This is not the usual story of a teen suffering the effects of disorder, but rather of a fascinating teen sharing her interesting and insightful summer experience.

NOTES

1. James Patterson and Hal Friedman, *Med Head: My Knock-Down, Drag-Out, Drugged-Up Battle with My Brain* (New York: Little, Brown, 2010).

2. Suzanne Crowley, "Up for Discussion: The Voices of Autism: A Look at Some Recent Books About Autism and the People Who Write Them," *School Library Journal* (2009): 18.

3. Tim Page, *Parallel Play: Growing Up with Undiagnosed Asperger's* (New York: Doubleday, 2009), 3.

4. Francisco X. Stork, *Marcelo in the Real World* (New York: Arthur A. Levine Books, 2009), 23, 54, 55.

5. Marc Tyler Nobleman, "The Boys of Steel and Asperger's Syndrome," *Noblemania: The Stories behind the Stories I Write*, October 22, 2010, http://noblemania.blogspot.com/2010/10/seeing-jerry-siegel-and-joe-shuster-in.html.

6. Nora Raleigh Baskin, *Anything but Typical* (New York: Simon & Schuster Books for Young Readers, 2009), 4–5, 14.

7. Suzanne Crowley, telephone interview with the author, March 21, 2011.

8. New Orleans librarian, e-mail to the author, August 2011.

seven

Stories of Support and Separation

Family Needs

Special needs family members have needs of their own. The one who is afflicted with an emotional trauma, mental illness, or physical or psychological challenge is not the only one affected. The family dynamics and demands are different for all and are not the typical topic of conversation. The tendency is for people to turn away and politely ignore a mom with a special needs child, to focus on something on the grocery shelf rather than make eye contact with a parent navigating her child's wheelchair down a too-narrow aisle. There's an ingrained sense that good manners condone such avoidance. The scolding "don't stare" that many of us grew up with still rings in our ears. Part of our hesitancy is the basic courtesy of respecting a family's privacy. Another part is ignorance and awkwardness about how to help. Stories about special needs people and their families that tell about strangers becoming involved, that show people who take risks and show compassion—these stories help to bring down the obstacle of social correctness and breach the barriers that such manners impose. Sometimes it's as simple as making eye contact, nodding, or saying hello.

While family members want to be included in community events, they do have a different row to hoe. While they listen to others speak about children going off to sporting events, their academic endeavors, and their participation in theatrical and performing arts or musical camps, oftentimes their own child may be in an extremely different stage of development or ability. For their child, such activities as being able to speak clearly, being able to socialize with another person, or doing something as unmentionable as keeping a meal down can be major accomplishments.

Some of the most helpful books and stories are those that take a snapshot of the whole family, because even in the most rock-solid situations, we see only a part of the picture. Stories allow you in. A mom may not gloat about how her son was able to spend an entire class in the classroom (as opposed to being sent for a time-out, as is his usual routine), or a dad might not brag about his daughter being home from rehab and gaining five precious pounds on her skeletal frame. These accomplishments, while huge within the household, aren't celebrated during social chitchat.

How do the siblings of special needs individuals feel when up against the conspicuous, if guarded, amount of attention their brothers and sisters receive? Some "normal" children keep their special needs family members a secret. Their brother is not the high school soccer star, music scholarship recipient, or English short-story award winner. Their sister may be in a special education class, homeschooled, in a therapeutic rehab facility or attending an alternative school. Their parents may have an illness, a physical disability, or a substance abuse issue. Who knows what hides behind a child's competent and well-adjusted façade? These children have needs of their own that aren't so easy to peg. Schools are filled with systems that run like clockwork. Within busy average school communities, conversation about special needs family members can be sensitive and uncomfortable. There are also the legal issues of confidentiality and privacy rights. The topic of special needs is often as overlooked and as isolated as the special education classrooms are. Considering and discussing literary characters who are challenged by family dysfunction or a sibling's special need is a way to connect to an otherwise avoided subject.

Cynthia Lord describes where the idea for her book *Rules* came from:

> My son has autism. One day when my daughter was about ten-years old she asked me, "Mom, how come I never see families like mine in books and on TV?" . . . I went looking for children's books that included characters with severe special needs. I did find some, but most of the books I read seemed very sad to me. Sadness is part of living with someone with a severe disability, but it's only one part. It can also be funny, inspiring, heartwarming, disappointing, frustrating—everything that it is to love anyone and to live in any family.[1]

Our overly sensitive respect for the privacy of such families makes sharing these fictionalized stories and personal memoirs essential. There certainly are times when becoming personal with family members is an invasion of privacy or an intrusion. Our media exposure to "TMI—too much information" has desensitized us and permits an unwritten license to pry. In Gary Schmidt's novel *Trouble,* his protagonist sees it this way:

Henry's mother, who did not want to be consoled by Sanborn's mother but who endured it all pretty well . . . Until they drove away, when his mother sighed, and sighed again, and then began to wonder aloud why everyone in Blythbury-by-the-Sea thought it was their right to know every little detail about Franklin's accident and every little detail about how he died and every little detail about how they were living now and when would they all finally stop asking how she felt because it wasn't their concern, anyway, because it was a private family matter.[2]

There is a fine line between respect for recovery and reaching out to support someone in a difficult situation. The beauty of story is that it can be intimate, personal, and private with many readers. Stories do not crassly broadcast misfortune but re-create a situation that a reader may comfortably experience and empathize with. Through a sensitively told story, the reader is able to respectfully peer in to learn about differences, dysfunction, and trauma, and perhaps perceive situations with more awareness and compassion.

Family Tales

Realistic stories often show how parents and siblings are anxious to help the at-risk family member, but their efforts are often rejected and they feel a sense of failure. The family stress may turn to dysfunction. Family members take on the overwhelming responsibility of figuring out how to help, how to protect, where to seek help. They may also feel compelled to keep a family secret. Family members might erect a façade of denial; they excuse away the evidence of trauma and as a result may end up enablers. A troubled teen, while frequently the focus of media exploitation, is not the child who fits into neat social circles that exude wholesome family relationships. It makes me think of Jeannette Walls's autobiographical *The Glass Castle*, a story in which the children are saddled with the responsibility of covering up for their parents' bizarre negligence. A shield of normalcy is how children and teens protect themselves; they hide their family differences and pretend that everything is perfect. These children hold up well to a standard assessment of "normal." They fit in. They don't cause trouble or demand attention. But they carry an awful lot of responsibility under their self-assumed role as protector. Reading stories that embrace the reality of physical, emotional, and learning differences may bridge a void in their personal misconceptions, fears, or discomfort. They may accept their own family's differences and realize that their family is not so odd or imperfect because *normal* fits very few families after all.

A school faculty member explained her experience as the "one who is okay" (i.e., normal) when she wrote about her reaction to Laurie Halse Anderson's *Wintergirls*:

> My anger at the novel ironically comes from Lia's unilateral perspective, the same perspective that makes the novel so realistic and powerful. My own experience with anorexia is . . . as the healthy one, one of the ones left behind. For the past ten years, my little brother has had an ongoing battle with anorexia, a struggle that led to a long-term hospitalization and a weight that plummeted to 57 pounds and still hovers below 100. He was sent home from college for being too sick. Similarly, my mother struggles with anorexia as part of a complex system of mental illness. For me this novel was very close to home. When Lia describes sitting in a group therapy session, I know exactly what that is like, except for the fact that I'm on the other side. I found myself getting angry with Lia in the same way that I got angry with my brother, or my mom. My position as a sibling of someone who nearly died from not eating made it nearly impossible for me to sympathize solely with Lia. When she kept rejecting the help from her mother I was thinking, "JUST LISTEN TO HER!" One of the greatest areas of interest for me in literature is that which deals with siblings and illness, for it seems that there is pain and destruction attached to being the sick one (obviously) but also, more subtly, to being the one who survives; the one who is okay.[3]

I recall Elisa's father's words, "I'm not looking for sympathy; empathy is a good word."

Suggested Reading

Sonnenblick, Jordan
Drums, Girls, and Dangerous Pie
Scholastic Press, 2005   Grades 7–12
cancer, family issues, guilt

Steven is a confident eighth grader, a solid student, and an ace drum player. He's probably the best drummer in the high school, which feeds his healthy ego, encourages practice, and keeps him focused. When Steven's 5-year-old brother, Jeffrey, gets really sick, his entire family life is turned upside down. Mom leaves her job in order to transport Jeffrey to his many hospital visits in the faraway city. Dad lapses into an emotional freeze zone. Jeffery, cursed with the effects of leukemia and the resulting treatment, is shaken but not destroyed. Steven pretends that everything is normal, except that he's practicing his drums obsessively, he's bargaining with God, and his once-steady schoolwork is plummeting. Steven's solace is his music, but his devil is the guilt of being healthy. No matter what he does, or thinks, he can't escape his raging conscience. Steven's narrative is a vivid peek into the thoughts of the overlooked healthy sibling. His endless concern for his brother, as well as his surface ability to enjoy the daily life of eighth grade—complete with hot girls and music performances—is painfully realistic. Many times you will laugh at Steven's chronic self-deprecating honesty. This story is more about love than pain. It is nakedly candid, guileless, and brave.

Appelt, Kathi
Kissing Tennessee and Other Stories from the Stardust Dance
Harcourt, 2000   Grades 7–12
dysfunctional family, abuse, date rape, death

Interrelated stories under the romantic guise of starry-eyed teens at their school dance, peppered with dark corners and scary shadows. A religiously tyrannical father equates lipstick with hell, a boy questions his sexual orientation and thus his friendships, the shattering aftermath of date rape is portrayed, and the acceptance of a too-early death is detailed. A little book dusted in romance and dusted off by stark reality.

Additional Titles of Interest Featured in Other Chapters

Park, Barbara
Mick Harte Was Here
Knopf, 1995   Grades 5–12
death in the family

Mick isn't wearing his bike helmet when he is hit and killed by a truck. This is not a mawkish story about death but the slow healing and recovery of the family left behind. Through his 13-year-old sister's narrative, this book celebrates a very funny boy's too-short life. This is a slight story that has a poignant and memorable impact for readers. It reads aloud well.

Fox, Paula
Radiance Descending
DK Ink, 1997   Grades 5–8
Down syndrome, denial, overachievement

Seven-year-old Paul is not all that impressed when newborn Jacob is brought home from the hospital. And his indifference turns to misgiving when his grandfather eyeballs him and delivers the news that Jacob is "different." So begins this slight yet powerful story of how Paul exists in a household that revolves around the needs of a younger brother with Down's syndrome. Little brother Jacob adores Paul and everything that he has and does. Paul grows up feeling that Jacob is the wedge that comes between Paul and everything else, especially their family's attention. Paul feels like the invisible son. Grandpa is a steady partner, but Paul also harbors jealousy of Grandpa's attention toward Jacob. He tries to repress the feeling and continues to enjoy their time together. The strength of this story lies in the genuine emotions of jealousy, anger, and spiteful resentment that Paul tangles with.

The book follows Paul and Jacob as they grow older, Paul excelling at school and Jacob making little developmental progress. Jacob worships Paul, who continues to feel irritated, disgruntled, and often angry toward his brother's behavior. The unrelenting personal conflict that Paul wrestles with—real feelings that bring him shame—are never overshadowed by pity for Jacob, who stands on his own, doing what he is capable of. It takes a subtle shift of awareness to realize that though Jacob's condition is demanding on the whole family, it doesn't mean that Paul is any less a part of the family. The radiance of this book is being saturated in Paul's wallowing. While it is intense and self-absorbed, it is also very real and understandable. Paul does not come off as a sour, selfish brat but as a sibling suffering the conflicts of a family challenge.

NOTES

1. Cynthia Lord, *Rules* (New York: Scholastic Press, 2006), 203.

2. Gary D. Schmidt, *Trouble* (New York: Clarion Books, 2008), 133.

3. Sarah Hoffman, faculty journal, s.v. January 2010.

eight

Beyond Special Needs

Just Read Good Stuff

Reading dissolves limitations and opens possibilities. There are times when you just can't imagine which book will touch a reader. Be sure to value the story content, story quality, personal connection, interest, and readability more than the prescribed educational standards and suggested reading levels. Don't cheapen the reading experience for children with reading disabilities by giving them watered-down stories with simple vocabulary. Chances are they know the meaning of the words, but it's the puzzle of the letter combinations that trips them up. Or it may be the simple fact that the story isn't interesting enough to hold their attention. The pleasure of reading what they enjoy will naturally develop into stronger reading skills. Linda Sue Park, speaking at the American Association of School Librarians Author Breakfast, shared this anecdote about making assumptions about kids' reading capabilities:

> A boy came to one of my signings. He was about 13 or 14 years old, a skater
> dude, long hair, baggy shorts, with a skateboard under his arm. His name was
> Luke, and his mother told me that he had a reading disability and had never
> once finished a book on his own. A librarian gave him one of my books. He not
> only finished it but read it again and again. Altogether, he read it four times.
> And then he went on to read other books. His mother told me candidly that
> he would never be a superstar reader, but because of my book, he had stopped
> seeing the printed word as the enemy. Well by this time, she was crying, I was

crying, and poor Luke was standing there clearly wishing he could ride his skateboard many miles away from both of us. Then he handed me the book to sign. It was *When My Name Was Keoko*. Of all my books, it is by far the most difficult, both structurally and in subject matter. If you had told me about a kid like Luke, it is the last book of mine I would have given him.[1]

Give children books that will snag their interest. Respect their intelligence, their right to choose, and their inclination to pursue the story. If the story is worth pursuing, chances are strong that a reader will accept the challenge.

Advocate popular books that are dismissed as "not real books." Choice selections include *Guinness Book of World Records, Guinness Book of Sport Records, Calvin and Hobbes*, the DK Eyewitness book series, *Where's Waldo?, Harry Potter, Magic Eye, Magic Eye Fantastical Optical Illusions* pop-up books, and graphic novels. The Maximum Ride, Alex Rider, and 39 Clues series are action-packed into short, easy-to-get-into chapters. James Patterson, author of the Maximum Ride series, said of his books, "I don't want the person to get up before I'm done telling my story. My stories are economical, compact, and concise."[2] These are books that children with—and without—special needs enjoy. They are leisure reading. The appeal includes the white space on the page, a generous amount of illustrations, page-turning action, short chapters, zany humor, and in the case of pop-up books, physical interaction. If kids had coffee tables in their rooms, these would be the books scattered on them.

Magazines are an attractive and nonthreatening choice for leery readers, from *Highlights for Children* to *Rolling Stone*. Others include *Sports Illustrated for Kids, Transworld Snowboarding, World Soccer, Shonen Jump, Horse & Rider, Backpacker, Odyssey, Discover, Popular Science*—if your child has a special interest, chances are there's a special interest magazine suited for him or her. Magazines have plenty of diverse subject matter, developmental interest ranges, and reading levels for all.

Find Out What Kids Like

Watch and consider what books they pick up on their own.

Ask students to keep a reader's journal. This might mean that they simply jot down the title and author of a favorite read. Or encourage them to write their reflections about the books that they are reading and to share their journal with you. Write a response to their thoughts. This is an effective and nonintrusive connection with students. Also, their candid book "reviews" may be an eye-opener about books that would not have otherwise been considered good matches.

Bookstores stay in business by being "in the know." Speak with local bookstores and find out what's hot in the children's and teens' sections. Privately owned bookstores are an indispensable resource. They have publishers feeding them the buzz on the top new titles and handing off advance reader's copies.

Sponsored by the Library of Congress, Letters about Literature (LAL) is an annual competition that encourages students to write to their favorite author. Customize the competition's extensive lesson plans to work with your students. LAL is an avenue for children to write candidly to an author who has touched their lives. Learn how students feel about their favorite books through their letters.

Recently I had a conversation with a 12-year-old girl who lost her dad to cancer the year before. Her brother was in an alternative boarding school, her mother worked long hours, her grandparents were helping as much as possible. I asked the girl about her favorite book and without hesitation she said, "*Girl Overboard*. In that book the girl says, 'I feel as though I'm drowning,' and because of everything that was going on in my life, I felt that way too. It really helped me." She participated in the LAL in her English class and wrote to Justina Chen Headley about how *Girl Overboard* resonated with her.

The following example is how I learned more about one student's reading interests as a direct result of the LAL program. My student had a reading disability, and he rarely discussed books; he was reticent to participate in the LAL project. He was shy and nervous about not having an author he connected with. Finally, bravely, he came up to me and asked if he could write to Jeff Smith. He wrote this letter:

> When I was seven I first found *Bone*. Normally I don't get into books or finish them but when I read *Bone* it was something different. It was interesting and I wanted to read it. It has everything; the plot, characters and pictures too. I liked how the brothers were funny and friendly. Sometimes the brothers wanted to kill each other, which I got because I have a sister who sometimes drives me crazy. Other times they are best friends, which is also like me and my sister. I related to Bone because he had to go to a new valley. I had to leave my old school and come to a boarding school. I felt like Bone, we both had to endure the hardest winter in our lives.

A vulnerable letter from a shy boy who worried whether the graphic novel he enjoyed and identified with was good enough to be considered "real" reading.

What to Recommend

It cannot be said often enough: foremost, match a reader's interest to the story's content. Recommend children's and young adult (YA) titles for the most delightful reasons of all—pleasure and relaxation.

If a child is seeking a source of identity and empathy, you might look for specific themes. Consider the particular type and extent of the disability or disorder, and select stories with themes of self-acceptance, survival, and resolution.

Humor often teases out discomfort and soothes tender wounds. Laughter is a gentle tonic. Introduce books that make everyone laugh. The following book recommendations are highly readable and entertaining. They are funny, or action packed, or adventurous—and all are page-turners. They are the books that one student reads and an undercurrent of interest begins. Next thing you know there's a steady stream of students eager to read. Popular reads are a persuasive way to encourage kids to read.

Suggested Reading

Kinney, Jeff
Diary of a Wimpy Kid series
Amulet, 2007   Grades 4–8

Greg is in conflict: he wants to do the right thing, but status, girls, and a dried-up piece of cheese on the playground (cursed with the Cheese Touch) get in the way. Nothing's simple or sensible in middle school; Greg's good intentions seem sabotaged at every turn. Very funny graphic novels.

Headley, Justina Chen
Girl Overboard
Little, Brown, 2008   Grades 7–12

After a snowboarding accident, a billionaire's daughter must rehabilitate both her knee and her self-esteem while forging relationships with those who accept her for who she is.

Sachar, Louis
Sideways Stories from Wayside School
Follett, 1978   Grades 3–5

With silly word play, scary teachers, kind janitors, and floors that don't exist, here is a wacky school where kids have fun. Students often recall the Wayside School series as "the funniest books I ever read."

Park, Barbara
Skinny-Bones
Yearling, 2006   Grades 3–5

Alex is a puny athlete with a big mouth. Baseball is his game, but it's his smart-aleck attitude that steals the show.

Spinelli, Jerry
Stargirl
Knopf, 2000   Grades 4–7

Dancing to her own music and charming those around her, Stargirl's free spirit is a wonderful gift not to miss. A study in the power of being a nonconformist in middle school—where conforming and popularity are the status quo. This story has a magic that lasts long after it is over.

Blume, Judy
Tales of a Fourth Grade Nothing
Dutton, 1972   Grades 3–5

Fudge is 2 years old and loaded with trouble. His older brother, Peter, is absolutely certain that Fudge will ruin his life. And, to some extent, he's right.

Various authors
The 39 Clues series
Scholastic, 2009   Grades 4–8

Written by a who's who of today's young adult and children's fiction—Rick Riordan, Linda Sue Park, Gordon Korman, to name just a few. A brother-sister team is racing against others to discover clues hidden around the world; plot-heavy and action-packed adventures are solved with the help of the reader.

Riordan, Rick
The Red Pyramid
Disney/Hyperion, 2010   Grades 6–8

As with Percy Jackson and the Olympians series, Riordan does a great job of meshing humor with action and adventure. This time it's all about Egyptian mythology. Riordan's fans won't be disappointed.

Selznick, Brian
The Invention of Hugo Cabret: A Novel in Words and Pictures
Scholastic Press, 2007   Grades 4–12

Highly illustrated story offering multiple levels of literary pleasure. An orphan living in a clock tower survives by wit and stealth and sets free a sophisticated and ingenious chain of imaginative events. Filled with intrigue, adventure, and suspense. The exquisite black-and-white illustrations stand alone for younger children who enjoy visual storytelling. (*Hugo*, the movie directed by Martin Scorsese and released in 2011, was based on this book).

Additional Titles of Interest Featured in Other Chapters

Big Nate: In a Class by Himself (chapter 3, page 22)

Hidden Talents (chapter 3, page 26)

Joey Pigza Swallowed the Key (chapter 3, page 27)

The Lightning Thief (chapter 3, page 28)

Space Station Seventh Grade (chapter 9, page 135)

The Strange Case of Origami Yoda (chapter 6, page 100)

Wonderstruck: A Novel in Words and Pictures (chapter 5, page 73)

Korman, Gordon
Chasing the Falconers
Scholastic, 2005   Grades 4–8

A fast-paced, action-packed adventure that fans of the Alex Rider and Maximum Ride series will read in one sitting. After their parents are thrown in jail for treason, a brother and sister are placed in the care of a juvenile detention facility for their own safety. A chance escape leads them on a dangerous cross-country adventure to prove their parents' innocence. If you hate reading but love TV, this one's for you!

Smith, Jeff
Bone: Out from Boneville (Bone series)
Scholastic, 2005   Grades 4–8

The Bone cousins are banned from their home of Boneville and are swept up in an epic adventure in a whole new world. A wonderful place of royalty and dragons, but evil forces must be battled. Heroic and idyllic, these books fly off the shelf. Graphic novel/comic format.

Meyer, Stephenie
Twilight series
Little, Brown   Grades 8–12

Vampires, werewolves, damsels in distress, gothic romance—who can resist? Teen readers (especially females) won't come up for air until they're finished with this series.

Collins, Suzanne
The Hunger Games series
Scholastic   Grades 7–12

A postapocalyptic world where a government-sponsored voyeuristic thrill is the entertainment that determines the success of individual land provinces. Take the survivor series idea, crank it up, have a smart, strong female hero, throw kids into gladiator teams, add a dash of romance, top it off with a fight-to-the-death climax, and you've got a winner.

~~~~~~

Rowling, J. K.
Harry Potter series
Arthur A. Levine   Grades 4–12

If you haven't heard about this one, you're too sheltered. In my mind, the best thing about the series—aside from the endearing and enduring cast of characters and the creative and imaginative world they live in—is that parents get excited and talk to their kids about these books.

~~~~~~

Rennison, Louise
Angus, Thongs and Full-Frontal Snogging: Confessions of Georgia Nicolson
HarperCollins, 2000   Grades 7–9

Georgia Nicolson is bursting with angst and attitude. Nothing is safe from her candid view of the dull life that surrounds her and the exciting life that escapes her. The British dialect adds edge and hilarity.

Westerfeld, Scott
Uglies
Simon Pulse, 2005   Grades 8–12

Everybody is supermodel gorgeous and having fun. What's wrong with that? Plenty!

~~~~~~

Patterson, James
The Final Warning: A Maximum Ride Novel
Little, Brown, 2008   Grades 7–9

A smart, fast-paced adventure yarn that every Maximum Ride fan will rip through.

~~~~~~

Patterson, James
The Dangerous Days of Daniel X
Little, Brown, 2010   Grades 5–9

Daniel X is an extraterrestrial on a mission to avenge his earth family, who have been murdered by intergalactic criminals. Time travel, apparitions, and a hardy amount of action and imagination keep the surprises rolling for the reader.

WEBSITE RESOURCES FOR FURTHER RESEARCH
AND RECOMMENDED READING

Books for Boys
www.talestoldtall.com/B4B.html

Michael Sullivan has done the research, has the facts, and best yet, knows why and what boys want to read.

Good Comics for Kids

http://blog.schoollibraryjournal.com/goodcomicsforkids/

School Library Journal, a reputable resource for school librarians, offers up an informative blog devoted to a variety of comics and graphic novels. Up-to-date information on what's happening in the graphic novel market, as well as the most current reviews.

Graphically Speaking

www.voya.com/tags/graphic-novels/

Voice of Youth Advocates (VOYA) offers the column "Graphically Speaking" by graphic novel expert Kat Kan. Kan lists the top graphic novels of the year.

Great Graphic Novels for Teens

www.ala.org/yalsa/ggnt/

YALSA's (Young Adult Library Services Association) annual list of the top graphic novels for ages 12–18.

Guys Read

www.guysread.com

The website from Jon Scieszka, the guru of getting kids laughing and having fun reading. A site that's dedicated to getting the least likely readers in the family to read: the boys!

Read Kiddo Read

www.readkiddoread.com

James Patterson's motivational site to encourage popular must-reads for kids. Easy to navigate, organized by reading and high-interest level, and complete with numerous contemporary reading lists.

NOTES

1. Linda Sue Park, speech, author breakfast, American Association of School Librarians (AASL) conference, Charlotte, NC, November 8, 2009.

2. James Patterson, "Turbocharge Your Day with James Patterson! Read Kiddo Read! Parents and Librarians Band Together to Make Kids Lifelong Readers" (speech), AASL conference, Charlotte, NC, November 6, 2009.

nine

Special Delivery—Stories for All

Calling Attention to Special Titles for Children and Young Adults

Y ou can learn an awful lot about people through literature. Educators who promote books about real-life situations, with realistic special needs characters, their families, and their friends, help reveal the invisible and merge it into the mainstream. Just as we teach about multiculturalism, our other differences—psychological, physical, emotional and medical conditions—require equal time. As with multiculturalism, this is done with deliberate and intentional delivery. Special needs individuals are legally acknowledged but all too often culturally ignored. And as special needs people may be overlooked, there is a lot of great books about them that are overlooked. You can't depend on the media or the publicity generated from trendy best sellers to routinely highlight special needs protagonists; such books may need your special delivery. Whether by bulking up your collection, talking about these books, having authors visit, or creating programming, awareness won't happen without time investment and exposure. There are a variety of ways to call attention to stories outside our typical circles.

Readers often reach for what they're familiar and comfortable with. A book about diverse living situations is not always a hot-ticket choice. Stories about children with learning differences, physical disabilities, or psychological challenges need introduction into the mainstream. This is not a one-person mission but a whole school's intentional advocacy for awareness. If you are able to represent and advocate for the novels, there's a good chance that English departments will embrace and include them. Below are some strategies to help.

Booktalking

Booktalking is when you verbally present a short description of the book to an audience—this is one of the most immediate, personal, and convincing ways to promote a book. If you like a story, you'll give it a winning sell when you talk about it. You can take your mission to the classroom, faculty meeting, or department meetings; give a school board or library board presentation, or workshop; or take it straight into a student's home (as I did with Elisa). All you need is your enthusiasm and some index cards with bullet points about the book, and you're set.

I am going to risk calling attention to an educational practice that every faculty member dreads: the interminable end-of-the-school-year faculty meetings. Here's the beauty of it: while the faculty is held hostage, this is the perfect opportunity to commandeer some booktalk time. Present good summer reads that will entertain as well as have the potential to be used in next year's curriculum. Have several copies of the books available for staff to check out for the summer. Tweak the presentation with visuals—PowerPoint slides of book covers—and make attendance irresistibly delicious by having good stuff to eat. Another effective time for such a presentation is the back-to-school orientation meetings. Lobby hard to wedge booktalk time into the faculty meeting schedule—at the end, at the beginning, or in the midst of the school year. The positive results are well worth it. There will be many books read and used in the curriculum as a direct result from this delivery.

For professional pointers on how to present booktalks, here are some resources that include booktalk summaries:

Baxter, Kathleen A., and Marcia Agness Kochel. *Gotcha Again! More Nonfiction Booktalks to Get Kids Excited About Reading.* Greenwood Village, CO: Libraries Unlimited/Teacher Ideas Press, 2002.

———. *Gotcha Good! Nonfiction Books to Get Kids Excited about Reading.* Westport, CT: Libraries Unlimited, 2008. Also *Gotcha Covered!*, and *Gotcha for Guys!.* All are probably as good as it gets.

Bodart, Joni Richards, and H. W. Wilson Company. *Index to the Wilson Booktalking Series: A Guide to Talks from Nine Volumes.* New York: H.W. Wilson, 1997. Booktalks produced by Bodart over the years, including the Booktalking the Award Winners series.

Bromann, Jennifer. *Booktalking That Works.* New York: Neal-Schuman Publishers, 2001. A wealth of information about booktalking methods, as well as plenty of sample booktalks.

Jones, Patrick. *Connecting Young Adults and Libraries: A How-to-Do-It Manual*. New York: Neal-Schuman Publishers, 1998. Includes a chapter on booktalking, including "hooks" and several sample booktalks.

Littlejohn, Carol. *Keep Talking That Book! Booktalks to Promote Reading*. Worthington, OH: Linworth, 2000. Designed to help librarians and teachers promote reading through booktalking. Loaded with booktalks and various indices to help users locate talks by age, genre, and so on.

THE RESULTS OF BOOKTALKING TO YOUNG READERS

I was invited to talk up books for fourth-, fifth-, and sixth-grade students at a private school library. The purpose was to showcase titles that kids would love to read. Tucked in my pile of surefire reads were *Rules* and *Out of My Mind*. One is the story about a young girl living with a younger brother who is autistic; the other is about 11-year-old Melody, who has a powerful affinity for words but is unable to speak. After the booktalks children eagerly looked over the action-packed-adventure and comical stories—*The Lightning Thief, Diary of a Wimpy Kid,* and the like. No surprise here. The surprise was how many students asked to borrow *Rules* and *Out of My Mind*. I left my copies with the students' librarian, and a waiting list began. The owner of the local bookstore, who also was in attendance, saw the student interest and added the two titles to her next order. The unsolicited reaction from these students broke down preconceived notions: children want to know about one another. Certainly they enjoy a fast-paced escape novel, a fantasy series, an adventure tale, and a laugh-out-loud story, but they are also interested in—and receptive to—learning about what life is like for others, from all walks of life.

Without the introduction of a booktalk, young readers might not know of some very inspirational and captivating stories. A well-written sensitive story portraying life as it is for their special needs peers is a comfortable window. It is an invitation to consider people who may look different but have similar feelings. We segregate children into their special classrooms, resource centers, or learning labs to help support and assist them. But within a school community students are frequently shuttered out by their differences. Michael Sullivan points out that boys are especially vulnerable. In 1994, 85 percent of special education students in American were male, and 70 percent of children in remedial classes were male.[1] Sometimes our well-intentioned support systems insulate kids *away* from the community.

Through the stories told in books, children who feel different and alienated may be comfortably reconnected, understood, and accepted. This is not to turn the classroom into a counseling session but to provide an opportunity for character study, plot construction, and literary analysis. For the sake of continuity, I'll use Jack Gantos's character Joey Pigza as a concrete example of a special needs individual who portrays universal sensitivities. (Spoiler alert: I'll be giving the end of the series away in this section.) Many of the conflicts that Joey wrestles with, while certainly different, are accentuated problems that we all contend with: family issues, mistrusting our instincts, controlling our impulses, questioning others' motives, embarrassment, feeling unpopular and excluded, being powerless, and on and on.

Joey has ADHD. His home life is dysfunctional—Grandma suffers from ADHD and is a negligent caregiver, and his single mom loves Joey but is overwhelmed with work and continues to struggle with advances from her estranged husband. Meanwhile, Dad sabotages Mom's efforts to keep Joey on his medication. Joey, all the while failing to balance his own behaviors, is positively crumbling from the weighty fallout of the adults in his life. By the story's end, Mom successfully keeps Dad out of their life, and Joey realizes that taking his medication helps control his impulsivity and compulsive behavior. Instead of being the class clown and becoming a social misfit, he learns the satisfaction of personal accomplishment and the enjoyment of friendships. Not so very different from how most of us feel when overcoming personal adversity.

Special Author Visits

Having an author visit your school or the public library is a very successful way to promote books and reading. Visiting authors are really just another special guest performance at your school. If you select a great novel that pivots on a special needs character and then are fortunate to secure the author behind the story, you'll make a compelling case for the cultural and social benefits of such literature. When Jack Gantos came to our school he was ready to discuss his famously funny and infamously disruptive character, Joey, the little boy many of us are dealing with in our classrooms: impulsive, compulsive, the class clown, frustrating, and daunting. Because Gantos talked about Joey's issues with the faculty and students, there was further understanding and empathy for what hitherto had been intolerance and annoyance. Not all schools are able to afford author visits, but if yours can, do it. The meaningful difference it makes to student and faculty awareness is immeasurable.

Another direct connection and vital reaction came when Laurie Halse Anderson visited. One of my students wrote about Anderson's book *Wintergirls,* "This book helps teenagers realize how dangerous, even deadly, eating disorders can be, but [it] still helps them to realize that there is a way to recover." Another teen, serving on a panel with the author spoke about Anderson's book *Speak,* "I have felt the way Melinda does."

While I have never had a brutal experience like she did, I am often on the outskirts of the social scene." This student, diagnosed with high-functioning Asperger's syndrome, frequently remained cloistered in her own thoughts. A huge reader but hesitant to discuss interpersonal perspectives—she's a reluctant communicator. When she connects with characters and unabashedly articulates her own inner feelings, it underscores the value of literature and the relevance of author visits.

Read-Aloud Programming: The Reader Workshop

Listening to stories read in a group setting about people with differences helps dissolve fear, promotes understanding, and provides a natural time for discussion. If children are to enjoy reading, developing their literacy skills must be a supportive and positive experience. I believe that reading aloud is good for teenagers. Young adult literature has more than enough drama, trauma, and turbulence to go around. This makes YA lit a comfortable and welcome ally for our most apathetic and alienated students. Many special needs children are often isolated by the nature of their physical limitations and emotional fallout. They and their families are alienated from a culture that shies away from their differences. Reading aloud is a nonthreatening vehicle to present unusual situations, articulate differences, promote personal expression, and encourage response. Keep in mind the practicalities when organizing this programming; for example, the hearing-impaired student may need a signing teacher or interpreter to participate.

Reading aloud in a group environment is an effective way to talk about uncomfortable, controversial, and overlooked subject matter. ADD, ADHD, reading and learning disabilities, and other disorders disrupt a child's intellectual development and undermine their confidence. When stories are read aloud, they're delivered intentionally into the mainstream classroom; since listening is done as a group, this also helps dissolve the label of "struggling independent reader." (Research proves that reading aloud promotes a natural transition from listening to stories to independently reading stories.[2]) Listeners can concentrate on the content, crisis, and resolution of a story and not feel frustrated if they're unable to decipher the scrambled and puzzling letters. Listening to stories being read aloud is an all-inclusive way to foster discussion. It is relaxing and best of all pleasurable. The beauty of the medium is that from the most academically inclined student to an academically struggling child, the stories are enjoyed equally and responded to differently. One ninth-grade student says, "I have a hard time paying attention. So hearing a story read out loud helps with my listening skills. It makes me want to read." Having conversations about the literature and discovering the different reactions and perspectives animate the experience. It's not so different from listening to music: if the composition appeals to a diverse audience, unity develops from the shared experience. Teens tell me that they enjoy the "group thing" of reading aloud. They say that it helps them look at the story differently when they listen to their peers talk about something that they haven't thought of.

Most teens are uncomfortable calling attention to themselves in the best of situations. But if they're contending with learning disabilities or physical, psychological, or emotional problems, they won't want their challenge to be the center of attention. A sensitive adult is able to ascertain whether a story line will provide a safe vantage point of discussion. Reading a story out loud and having follow-up group conversation initiates group awareness, confronts social schisms, may defuse shame, and demystifies the emotional differences between the perceived normal child and a special needs child.

Don't use reading aloud as a transparent guise to present stories that are solely about special needs individuals or their families. It is of foremost importance to select stories that read aloud well and will be enjoyed by all. The idea is to be all-inclusive and spark the group enjoyment of listening to a story. Should there be a special needs character in the mix, all the better, but don't limit stories to that criteria. Such a specific focus is unnatural and will make children uncomfortable. There are many great stories that all students identify with, and the ones that you love best will no doubt be the best ones to share.

MORE ABOUT WHY READING ALOUD WORKS

The following is a list of reasons that advocate for reading aloud during class time, from elementary right through high school.

- Reading aloud supports multiple intellectual capabilities, developmental needs, and learning styles. It welcomes struggling readers onto the same page as competent independent readers, encouraging discussion around story content and comprehension.
- Reading aloud dissolves the damaging barrier that separates the learning disabled and reluctant readers from mainstream classrooms of competent, independent readers.
- Reading aloud introduces sensitive subject matter—such as special needs—to a group. It provides opportunities to reflect and process through discussion. It may sensitively spur conversations about uncomfortable topics, and it provokes consideration and response.

- Reading aloud stimulates group discussions—from empathetic reflection to emotional resolution.
- Reading YA titles aloud is a user-friendly way to introduce overlooked titles.
- Reading aloud helps develop confidence and comprehension, from prompting self-reflection to communal awareness. In a nonthreatening way it draws the introspective or invisible child into the group.
- It encourages children to consider some of the obstacles that their classmates face.
- Boys in particular love read-aloud classes. One in three boys are in remedial reading classes by third grade. As educator Michael Sullivan so aptly states, "We've made being a boy a learning disability."[3] Furthermore, he spells out why some reluctant readers remain reluctant: "Boys learn that 'when I learn to read, people will stop reading to me.'"[4] Overwhelming statistics prove boys are left behind when secondary education demands independent reading from students—many of whom aren't ready to go it alone. Some of the most compulsive, impulsive, fidgety boys in our school arrive at the reader's workshop early and sit raptly attentive throughout the class period.
- In the introduction to his million-copy best seller *The Read-Aloud Handbook,* Jim Trelease writes, "Reading aloud to children improves their reading, writing, speaking, listening—and, best of all, their attitudes about reading. . . . A child hears a story on at least three different levels: intellectual, emotional and social. . . .Teachers who only have the opportunity to read to a group of slow, medium, and fast students should remember that, while those students may read and write on different levels, they usually listen on the same level."[5]
- Reading expert Stephen Krashen also points out that "there's almost the same language attainment from hearing [a book read] aloud as from reading [it] independently."[6]
- Teens love being read to!

When you consider the many different intelligences that a story read out loud appeals to, this is a valid reason in and of itself to encourage time for all-inclusive read-aloud classes. Since this is not a book about creating programming, I urge you to collaborate with English teachers and call their attention to the large scope and variety of special needs characters in today's quality literature. For an in-depth description on how to organize read-aloud programming, see my book *Reviving Reading: School Library Programming, Author Visits, and Books That Rock!* (Libraries Unlimited, 2006).

The following list includes titles that read aloud well. With any and all read-aloud material, read it yourself first. Think about how it will read out loud to your audience. Yes, you must think about your audience. Here's a cautionary tale: one day a sixth-grade English teacher came storming into the library asking how I could possibly recommend a particular Jack Gantos title. She had read a dicey section out loud to her class, literally—it had to do with a cat getting diced in a car engine. She had not reviewed the story first. She huffed, "That guy's a maniac!" Having previously reminded her to read these stories first, I had to ask, "Are you going to stop reading it?" "No, I can't now. The kids love it!" I gently reminded her to preview the next chapters first and she tossed back, "Good point!"

Don't count on reading aloud your favorite childhood literature—chances are it won't read out loud well and you (and your audience) will be disappointed. Long descriptive passages, while perhaps intellectually and aesthetically satisfying when read independently, are the kiss of death when reading aloud to teens. Look for short chapters, action, sharp dialogue, and far-fetched nonsense. Mystery, adventure, suspense, a little romance, and lots of humor are prime read aloud ingredients. Also novels-in-verse have lyrical tone, short phrases, lots of white space on the page (to encourage continued independent reading) and much read-between-the-lines inferences that contribute to successful follow-up discussion. Be sure to save time afterward for student responses.

Suggested Reading

Flagg, Fannie
Daisy Fay and the Miracle Man
Warner Books, 1992   Grades 7–12

A laugh-out-loud reminiscence of a young girl surviving the 1950s in Mississippi. For all the quirkiness of her surroundings, nothing can compare to her wacky father (who *doesn't* know best) and the wild escapades he gets them into.

Sachar, Louis
Holes
Farrar, Straus and Giroux, 1998   Grades 4–8

An enchanting story in which nothing is as it seems. Stanley Yelnats is accused of a deed he didn't do; he's sent to Camp Green Lake, a juvenile detention home in the midst of the desert, run by diabolical adults and governed by whispers from a mystical past that includes ancient folklore and hidden treasure. Don't miss this one!

Gantos, Jack
Jack Adrift: Fourth Grade without a Clue
Farrar, Straus and Giroux, 2003   Grades 4–6

The Jack Henry story cycles are weird, wacky, and full of wry humor. Featuring the author's alter ego, Jack Henry, they offer multiple levels for literary interpretation, comparison and discussion. This may be the most endearing of the stories, presenting Jack as an innocent, curious, and self-conscious nine-year-old trying to figure out the world around him. This title was praised by *Booklist* for its "hilarious, exquisitely painful, and utterly on-target depiction of the life of an adolescent and preadolescent boy."

Gantos, Jack
Jack on the Tracks: Four Seasons of Fifth Grade
Farrar, Straus and Giroux, 1999   Grades 6–8

Jack is mesmerized by all things gross. For English class he writes a short story about his friend's tapeworm about which one reviewer said, "This makes Thomas Rockwell's *How To Eat Fried Worms* seem like a picnic." Each interconnected chapter stands alone as a short reading. They range from the macabre to the hilarious and from the surreal to the quirky. Extreme graphic descriptions, which of course, kids love.

Gantos, Jack
Jack's New Power: Stories from a Caribbean Year
Farrar, Straus and Giroux, 1995   Grades 7–12

These story cycles stand alone as strong short stories. "Dynasty" begins as a rescue at sea before taking the distinctive Gantos dive into facing your fear. In "Purple," Mother wants chicken for dinner, and Jack and his brother are introduced by their Barbadian housekeeper to the game of "chase the headless chicken." Things go from bad to worse. Jack pulls out his own wart, thus ripening it for infection, and justifiably remains the butt of his sister's chronic biting comments. Family life underscores these stories, but pubescent imagination enlivens them.

Gantos, Jack
Rotten Ralph
Houghton Mifflin, 1976   Grades pre-K–4

Ralph is an incorrigible cat infamous for his nasty tricks and terrible traits—traits that underlie the shadows of our own worst selves. Sarah is his adoring caregiver who loves him unconditionally. Ralph makes his own life miserable and also wrecks havoc on hers. Ralph's temperamental behavior and Sarah's patient tolerance are a winning combination for young readers.

Kidd, Sue Monk
The Secret Life of Bees
Viking, 2002   Grade 8–adult

In the Deep South of 1964 Lily runs from her father's accusations of a horrid crime with a murky truth: he tells her that she pulled the trigger that killed her mother. Lily is haunted by questions of her guilt. Her life is further rocked by the glaring wrongs of racial inequity. She and her beloved black caregiver, Rosaleen, escape to Rosaleen's sisters' home, where the three nurturing women help to weave Lily's broken life back together.

Spinelli, Jerry
Space Station Seventh Grade
Little, Brown, 1982   Grades 6–8

Jason's life is a journey into the melodramatic and intense world of surviving seventh grade—from girls to gym showers, body hair, pimples, and dealing with the questionable advice from a best friend who seems high on testosterone.

McDonald, Janet
Spellbound
Frances Foster Books, 2001   Grades 8–12

Raven's aspirations of going to college are dashed when she becomes an unwed teen mom. A story where characters push back against personal adversity. Smart kids do

Additional Titles of Interest Featured in Other Chapters

King of the Mild Frontier: An Ill-Advised Autobiography (chapter 4, page 49)
The Lightning Thief (chapter 3, page 28)
Mick Harte Was Here (chapter 7, page 111)
Sideways Stories from Wayside School series (chapter 8, page 117)

stupid things, but they don't need to be ruined by them. Raven won't give up and works hard to overcome her troubles and achieve success.

Peck, Richard

The Teacher's Funeral: A Comedy in Three Parts

Dial Books, 2004 Grades 6–8

This book is as fun to read aloud as the story is hilarious. It begins, "If your teacher has to die, August isn't a bad time of year . . ." Filled with wisecracking country dialect and crazy country predicaments—including snakes in the outhouse—these big ol' country boys are riotous.

Creech, Sharon

Walk Two Moons

HarperCollins, 1994 Grades 5–9

A lovely story with parallel plot lines. Thirteen-year-old Salamanca takes a trip with her grandparents to retrace her disappeared mom's journey. She unrealistically hopes to find her mother before her birthday. Along the way we hear about Sal's friend Phoebe, whose mother also disappeared. Trouble is brewing, and while some events are predictable, others are a complete surprise. This charming intergenerational tale will make you smile as it also makes you cry. Newbery Award Winner.

Additional Titles of Interest Featured in Other Chapters

Athletic Shorts: Six Short Stories (chapter 3, page 21)
Kissing Tennessee and Other Stories from the Stardust Dance (chapter 7, page 109)
Owning It: Stories about Teens with Disabilities (chapter 6, page 97)
What Are You Afraid Of? Stories about Phobias (chapter 4, page 45)

SHORT STORIES THAT CAN BE READ
IN A SINGLE CLASS PERIOD

Grimes, Nikki
Bronx Masquerade
Dial Books, 2002   Grades 7–12

Multiple teen voices unmask pretense and reveal the depths of personal background, high school relationships, and individual makeup. These 18 poetry performances alternate in an open-mike style delivery. The creative format helps kids get into the groove of the three Rs: reading, 'riting, and rapping.

Gallo, Donald R., ed.
First Crossing: Stories about Teen Immigrants
Candlewick Press, 2004   Grades 7–12

A collection of multicultural contemporary stories by notable YA authors. David Lubar writes a tongue-in-cheek tale of a Transylvanian immigrant plunked into Alaska's dark zone. His new peers immediately suspect that he's a vampire and are afraid—all except for the goth girl, who of course finds this notion attractive. Other stories explore more serious aspects of immigration but are no less interesting.

Scieszka, Jon, ed.
Guys Write for Guys Read
Viking, 2005   Grades 6–12

A collection of short stories from some of the most notorious male writers of today's most-loved literature. Many offer autobiographical boyhood anecdotes, all written with the reluctant boy reading audience in mind. Short and fun.

Paulsen, Gary

How Angel Peterson Got His Name and Other Outrageous Tales about Extreme Sports

Wendy Lamb Books, 2003 Grades 6–8

Interrelated short story chapters that stand alone, linked by the high jinks of 13-year-old boys. From hang gliding with a World War II parachute, being trailed behind a speeding car to pioneer the sport of "extreme skiing," experimenting with being tossed over the local falls in a barrel, to landing in a stinking pigsty in the neighbor's farmyard, this book offers these outlandish and laugh-out-loud experiences.

Salisbury, Graham

Island Boyz: Short Stories

Wendy Lamb Books, 2002 Grades 8–12

Short stories that resonate with the culpability, vulnerability, and invincibility of youth. The unsettling "Doi Store Monkey" exposes the depths of lost innocence and the inherent cruelty of human nature. "The Ravine" is about a boy who honors his fear, stays safe in a precarious situation, and in exchange becomes socially ostracized.

Singer, Marilyn, ed.

Make Me Over: 11 Original Stories about Transforming Ourselves

Dutton Children's Books, 2005 Grades 8–12

Eclectic and literary, this collection explores the universal theme of escaping who we are to become someone else. From fantasy and sci-fi to realistic fiction, the appeal is a short story for anybody, about any body. Distress about body image, promiscuity, accomplishing goals, coming of age, dealing with an overbearing parent, or trying to shed the pangs of adolescence—it's all here.

Gallo, Donald R., ed.

No Easy Answers: Short Stories about Teenagers Making Tough Choices

Delacorte Press, 1997 Grades 8–12

These stories test the strength of teen moral conscience and ethical standards. Faced with blackmail, peer/parental pressures, drugs, unwanted pregnancy, and other hard conflicts, teens face consequences, take accountability for their actions, and learn that life doesn't come with an answer key.

Levithan, David

The Realm of Possibility

Knopf, 2004 Grades 7–12

A poetic mix of the yearning and the possibilities of youth. The distinct voice of a single narrator links together other voices in a daisy chain of events. The voices span from charming romantic daydreams to fretting over sexual identity and relationships—all the stories accentuated by the art of words placed just so. A book of simple lyricism with underlying emotional complexities.

NOTES

1. Michael Sullivan, *Connecting Boys with Books* (American Library Association, 2003), 3.

2. Jim Trelease, *The Read Aloud Handbook* (Penguin Books, 2006); Stephen Krashen, *The Power of Reading: Insights from the Research*, second edition (Libraries Unlimited, 1993), 78; Krashen, *Free Voluntary Reading* (Libraries Unlimited, 2011), 7, 40, 51; Sullivan, *Connecting Boys with Books*, 95–96.

3. Michael Sullivan, *Connecting Boys with Books 2: Closing the Reading Gap* (American Library Association, 2009), 19.

4. Michael Sullivan, "Connecting Boys with Books" (professional development workshop), Champlain Valley Educational Services, Plattsburgh, NY, 2007.

5. Jim Trelease, *The New Read-Aloud Handbook* (Penguin, 1999).

6. Stephen Krashen, *The Power of Reading: Insights from the Research* (Libraries Unlimited, 2006).

ten

Alternative Literary Options

t is a great moment for alternative literary choices. There are many reading alternatives for all and specific aids for people with special needs. A traditional book is no longer the only way, or the best way, to enjoy a story. Many claim that the book as we know it is soon to become obsolete. The old-fashioned book—pages bound together between two heavy-duty cardboard covers—will be enjoyed only by sentimental traditionalists, shelved as fond collectibles.

I am a sentimental traditionalist. I have good eyesight and am without reading disabilities. I'm one lucky individual. For those who read differently, there are many new ways to deliver the pleasure of story. In our modern age, literature availability is becoming increasingly all-inclusive.

Reading expert Michael Sullivan is an advocate for young boys who read differently. He explains that 30 years of national education research concludes,

> In every single test, in every single year, at every age, boys have tested lower than girls in their reading ability. The average boy is reading one-and-a-half years behind the average girl. We send kids to school to learn, and by the time they are in the 11th grade, the average American boy is reading three years behind the average American girl.

But, as Sullivan points out, "Children don't read to their reading level; they read to their interest level."[1]

Responding to my inquiry about alternative literature choices, one librarian writes:

> I want to mention strategy video games where there is a lot of reading
> involved (Pokémon and the Nintendo DS game Drawn to Life). Players have
> to type a word for whatever they need in the game; if they need to cross a body
> of water they could type in boat, canoe, wings, airplane, etc. My oldest child
> actually learned to read because of a Pokémon video game. He was in second
> grade and still could not really read. He got a Nintendo DS Pokémon game
> for Christmas and by the time the break was over he could read. The whole
> game is based on reading the text and making choices (it also taught him map
> skills). I find with a lot of kids with Asperger's it is finding the "thing" that
> makes them stop worrying about the process of reading and concentrate on
> the topic they are reading about. For my younger son, it was graphic novels
> that got him to read.[2]

There are multiple ways to access print media, from magazines to novels. The
content is the same, but the delivery is quite different. How it unfolds for the individual
is also different, but the marvelous fact is that it does figuratively unfold—sometimes
in an accessible, paperless way. It is truly a wonder. For Elisa, who is unable to focus
adequately on the small letters on a paper page, the electronic book makes a huge
difference. She is able to increase the font on her computer screen as well as select a
reading voice. She can choose a feature to have the computerized voice read as each
word is highlighted.

There are many ways to hear stories. Recorded books are available in a variety of
formats and offered from different suppliers. From downloading an audiobook to using a
screen reader to borrowing an MP3 version of a book, listeners may enjoy it on a Nook,
Kindle, iPod, iPad, or tablet—or they may pop an audio CD into a CD player. Some cars
have a USB port, so you may download several audiobooks onto a flash drive and listen
to them while you drive. There are now many alternative and feasible ways to access
literature. From children and young adults who struggle with independent reading to
those who are physically unable to hold a book, the digital age is a grand leveling field.

Libby Doan, former assistant head of academics at North Country School in Lake
Placid, New York, explains her reactions to using alternative reading devices with
students who have learning disabilities:

> I know that the Kindle was helpful to [one particular] student this year
> because it will read aloud, but what she really liked was being able to change

the size of the font on the screen. For someone with limited vision, this type of technology allows for large print reading. For a student who struggles with reading fluency, it allows him to "turn the page" more often and be less overwhelmed by the amount of text on the page. To be fair, it may be that the Nook or iPad also have these features, but the Kindle was what this student was using.

In my experience, audiobooks and reading alternatives protect a child's intellect, not stunt it.

I think that supporting fluency with audio options is critical—assuming the goal is to keep children engaged in a good story and love books. Developmentally, there is a moment when a child wants to "read it myself." For example, a typical bedtime reading progression goes something like this: the picture books change to chapter books and over time; the child reads to herself rather than being read to. A parent and teacher of a child who is still learning to read and/or read fluently needs to be aware that there is an emotional and developmental milestone related to the ability to read independently that exists in all students, including those who struggle with reading. These students benefit from reaching this milestone along with their more reading-able peers. Infusing a positive culture of audiobooks into the routine so that the child can "read before going to bed" or enjoy a good book while waiting in the doctor's office or when traveling supports the transition to independent reading. This tactic also allows access to age-appropriate, interesting literature, and provides the student with the same books as his or her peers—while still learning to improve reading skills in another mode.

It's also been my experience that reading struggles can be completely different than a child's ability to comprehend and think about books on a high level. Audiobooks can bypass the barriers of decoding, for example, to succeed in reaching higher order thinking and creative story-making. This is critical in the middle school years when abstractions, pulling out themes of stories, character analysis, and volume of work are all coming into play. A student may very well have the cognitive skill to tease out themes and understand books at a high level. Without audiobooks or other forms of reading, they will be stuck in the ACT or PROCESS of reading rather than processing the story in a way that develops abstract thinking, promotes healthy intellectual development, and supports their participation in classroom literary discussions.

This premise applies to textbooks as well. It is great to see the access to audio options growing. Early intervention with reading skills is critical and these alternatives to reading words off a page do not replace reading instruction and mastery. However, with sensitive timing and support, a child can keep their intellectual persona alive and growing—while continuing to strengthen and develop their reading skills.[3]

With technology changing at such a rapid rate, I'm certain of only one thing: only a small fraction of the progressive assistive features that are in use, marketed, and forthcoming are highlighted here.

Products and Services to Consider

Accessible Book Collection
www.accessiblebookcollection.org

The Accessible Book Collection provides high interest/low reading level digital text and e-books to qualified persons with disabilities. Students or individuals with a qualifying disability and nonprofit educational institutions may subscribe.

Audible.com
www.audible.com

This subscription service (now owned by Amazon.com) allows you to download books, magazines, and other recorded material to your iPod, iPhone, or MP3 player. Monthly or annual fee.

Bookshare: Accessible Books and Periodicals for Readers with Print Disabilities
www.bookshare.org

This website offers digital books, textbooks, periodicals, and other readings through a searchable online library. Bookshare members may download books, textbooks, and newspapers and access the material using adaptive technology. For students from the U.S. with a qualifying disability, membership is free due to funding from the U.S. Department of Education Office of Special Education Programs.

IDEAs That Work: Office of Special Education Programs (OSEP)
www.osepideasthatwork.org

Supported by the US Department of Education Office of Special Education Programs, this website offers "tool kits" for assessing students with disabilities as well as kits for teaching students with disabilities. For students, parents, and educators.

Learning Ally (formerly Recording for the Blind and Dyslexic)
www.learningally.org

"Making reading accessible for all," Learning Ally serves college and graduate students, veterans, and lifelong learners who are unable to read standard print due to blindness, visual impairment, dyslexia, or other learning disabilities. They have an educational audio textbook library featuring more than 70,000 downloadable titles in all K–12 curriculum areas. Materials are downloadable and accessible on mainstream as well as specialized assistive technology devices. Annual memberships are available for individuals and educational institutions.

National Library Service for the Blind and Physically Handicapped (NLS)— A Library of Congress Website
www.loc.gov/nls/

Through a national network of cooperating libraries, NLS administers a free library program of Braille and audio materials circulated—postage free—to eligible borrowers in the United States. This service has many children's and young adult literary recommendations, reputable lists, and titles available.

Read2Go
http://read2go.org

An e-book reader app available for readers with print disabilities, for purchase from Apple. Read Bookshare titles on the Apple iPad, iPhone, or iPod Touch.

Recorded Books on PlayAway
www.recordedbooks.com/index.cfm?fuseaction=school.playaway

Miniature digital self-contained audiobooks have a player inside, so they play aloud and don't need anything other than batteries and headphones. Students like them because they look like MP3 players. Unless otherwise noted, recordings are not adaptations and are narrated by talented "real people" readers. If applicable, have a hard copy of the book available to read along with. PlayAways may be plugged into a computer device, or speakers, for group audience listening. One downside to this product is that it runs on batteries—popular stories that circulate frequently will need battery replacements. PlayAways are pricey, but many libraries have them available for loan.

There is also the capacity to store entire personal libraries onto Kindles and Nooks. There are several attractive features on these e-book readers from the ability to increase the size of the font—a great asset for the visually impaired—to the fact that they are light—you can carry lots of books on a single e-reader device. And as of this writing, the Kindle DX features a text-to-speech function. One obvious downside to any of these e-readers is the need for a power source. Yet the market is competitive and the attractive assets—including increased battery life—are improving daily.

There is a variety of resources for students to access alternative media, media switching aids, and assistive technology. Many of them work a bit differently, but all of them present text as speech.

NOTES

1. Michael Sullivan, "Connecting Boys with Books" (professional development workshop), Champlain Valley Educational Services, Plattsburgh, NY, 2007.
2. New Orleans librarian, e-mail to the author, August 2011.
3. Libby Doan, North Country School, Lake Placid, New York, e-mail to the author, August 2, 2011.

eleven

Conclusion

Normal is a perspective defined by an individual viewpoint of what is "standard." More typically, it is what a culture embraces as acceptable behavior and protocol based on its status quo.

The most difficult part about wrapping things up for *Remarkable Books about Young People with Special Needs* is that there is always one more story to share, one more book to talk about. It is a blessing and a curse: a blessing because there are more and more stories that champion characters—and their families—who face down adversity to live fulfilling lives. A week doesn't go by when another novel claims my attention as worthy to include in this resource; a curse because at some point "the end" must come and thus, there are many good books that are not included here. If you bring up the subject of novels that feature a special needs individual or a family contending with dysfunction, people quickly offer up title suggestions. The interest—as much as the experience—is growing in our culture.

As I prepare to end this book I'll share one last story. This one is true, and it illustrates the bravery it takes to own up to having a disability.

A school superintendent in northern New York abruptly resigned without explanation. Members of the school district were curious about and uncomfortable with his sudden leave-taking. The school board was bombarded with questions but stayed silent. The media was all over what quickly became a hornet's nest of mystery and possible controversy. The worst was suspected. Finally the man came forward, explaining that he had bipolar disorder and needed to take time off to deal with his condition. In an interview with the local newspaper he described his struggle and the realization that he was unable to continue as superintendent. About the public nature of his personal situation he said, "I have given a lot of thought about public disclosure. I feel fine about it. I feel mental illness is not something society understands well and probably doesn't do well with." He concluded his interview saying, "Right now, what I would like to do is help people by sharing my story, and maybe people will become understanding and sympathetic toward people with the disease."[1]

The school superintendent's courageous admission was a significant contribution to his community. By honestly exposing his vulnerability, this man gives others strength. By accepting his disorder he will receive medical treatment and will stabilize. By hiding in shame, the disorder would manifest and chronically hijack his life. Not all secrets should be shared, but there is a difference between sensationalizing personal circumstance and admitting to a personal challenge. Any high-profile professional is at great risk in admitting personal disabilities or differences. In this case, while he'll regain his health, mental illness did cost the superintendent his job. Confronting obstacles takes guts.

Life is never as neat and predictable as we would hope. Sharing books and stories offers comprehension and compassion. Stories give companionship when we're lonely and acceptance when we're ashamed and prod humility when we're feeling overly confident by our good fortune of normalcy.

What's a Book Got to Do with It?

Stories about people who live with special needs connect us all, whether we as readers have similarities with the characters or not. The author tells part of the story, and the reader contributes the rest by reacting to what may, or may not be, implied. A single story, once it is read, becomes two stories. The author delivers it, and the reader interprets it according to his or her personal backdrop. It's a rewarding partnership, with no right or wrong. In the quiet contemplation of story, readers "read between the lines," pick up on voice inflections, nuance, inference, and connotation. The reader absorbs a character's personality, humor, pain, and unique experience. The reader's intuition elevates literature to a strange dimension that is palpable, sustainable, and experiential. The plot is the trail we follow we absorb and bond with the character. We all go through moments of feeling that we're the only one suffering a particular situation. Stories may not re-create an identical incidence, situation, or calamity, but when someone writes about challenge and survival or ups and downs, a camaraderie develops. As readers, we take vicarious falls and grab a literary safety line as the character who has captured us musters the heart to forge on.

Why get sidetracked about literature and intuition? Because this is why stories about people with differences are so instrumental and fundamental for us all. They connect us beyond a face-to-face conversation, beyond discomfort and preconceptions. In cases in which the character is an unreliable narrator because of mental illness, is misunderstood because of a disorder, is unable to speak without a communication board, is deaf, or is confined to a wheelchair and not often out among the community—in all these cases and so many more—stories are a solid source, perhaps the best source, to begin unlikely connections. For all their silent delivery, they trigger conversation. Take the novel *Freak the Mighty*, about a pair of oddball kids, both stricken with medical anomalies, who power through social misconceptions, gain personal awareness, suffer great loss, and are blessed with the eternal gift of friendship. Most kids won't pick up this story on their own, but if they read it in a classroom or book group, they'll never forget it.

Autism, Asperger's, and Unusual Thought Patterns and Behaviors

Tim Page, diagnosed with Asperger's syndrome as an adult, wrestles with the "outside the box" cliché. Galileo, Socrates, Mozart, Einstein, Michelangelo, Helen Keller, Madame Curie, Van Gogh, and other brilliant divergent thinkers and visionaries were probably considered unusual, enigmatic, quixotic, or quirky. These doers and thinkers would not have pursued their passion, made life-changing discoveries, or achieved original creations if they had settled into the conforming norm. This is not to say that we should teach to an uncivil and chaotic classroom. It is to point out that our efforts to harness the energy of our students, to push down the lid and guide independent minds to absorb uniform standards, seems questionable. While Anne Sullivan needed to tame the wild child Helen Keller, she did so for a purpose: to teach Helen language to express herself. ("First, last, and in-between, language. . . . Language is to the mind more than light is to the eye."[2])

Recently the Pulitzer Prize–winning poet Philip Schultz wrote about his brush with growing up "labeled" and being placed in the "dummy class." His third- and fourth-grade classes were torturous experiences. It was a time when there was little acknowledgment of learning differences and even less understanding of what that might mean. You were either smart or dumb. If you suffered from undiagnosed and misunderstood dyslexia, you were dumb. Schultz writes, "We know now that dyslexia is about so much more than just mixing up letters—that many dyslexics have difficulty with rhythm, meter and word retrieval, that they struggle to recognize voices and sounds."[3]

The more we dare to reveal our shortcomings, the more we will learn from one another.

The novels and memoirs recommended in this book offer reflection, understanding, and resolution. Sometimes they provide a window to recognize our own weaknesses and the inspiration to move forward. By reading about social "misfits" we are privy to characters with progressive, creative, and original thoughts; to positive attitudes pitting fortitude against the odds; and to willpower, discipline, and the optimistic courage it takes to face medical enemies that have no known cure.

Personal Reflection

As a young child I was shy and quiet. When I think back on the child who I was, there's no doubt I was a bit strange in my aloneness. Yet I remember great times and sometimes I long for that contented child. I didn't feel lonely. I had imaginary friends and an imaginary horse that I put away in her stall every night. My family always had pets. The dogs and I went about our business. I spent my days talking to them and teaching them tricks. Or I played on my own, roaming through the woods, claiming forts under willow trees, wading through brooks, or spending time reading—under the trees or off in a corner.

In first grade I chose my colors carefully and painstakingly colored inside the lines of my coloring book. I thought coloring inside the lines was what you were supposed to do in school, and I proudly brought my artwork to my teacher. The other children were grouped adoringly about her. I was unprepared for her response. She dismissed my efforts and asked why I didn't draw an original design instead of using a coloring book.

School was a nightmare. My elementary school classes seemed stocked with gifted children of the artistic and notable folks in the community. I was miserable and out of step among a confident crowd. I noticed that my drawings weren't good enough, I was the first one to sit down during a spelling bee, and I didn't have many friends; in a place with so many happy kids, I felt lonely. I thought I was the only one. I daydreamed my way out of the classroom only to end up *staying back*—the dreadful term of the time. I repeated fourth grade. Forty-plus years later this remains an embarrassing memory. It is also a difficult admission.

My days of pleasant naiveté were over. My brain played stories. It clamped shut at spelling, spiraled into panic at math, and snagged up uselessly while trying to retrieve historical facts or sort out political webs. While I may have appeared clueless, I was ever affected by the shame of feeling stupid. I was painfully self-conscious. My strong reading skills tamped down the red flags like wet blankets to fire. We moved a lot. Some school experiences were better, but none were great. Eventually I compensated, at first being the class clown, then feigning indifference, and finally becoming an underachiever. "I *can't* do it!" became my whine for attention.

My educational files don't show a classification of a learning disability, but I know what I know. We are all born with an Achilles heel, a weakness that we live with, hide, and eventually compensate for.

Through reading I connected with characters who overcame adversity. It was a comfort to discover that being different is normal. That *normal* really is a personal perception. That obstacles, instead of overwhelming a person, may serve to develop inner strength, confidence, and character. Characters who face challenges and conflict head-on are interesting and inspiring. They exude deep inner will and dogged personality. I respected them all. I vicariously absorbed their resilience and grit. I didn't want to be me, I wanted to be them! It took hundreds of stories but at some point there was an infusion of possibility from these motivational characters and a slight shift in my flawed and fragile confidence.

In the End

Obviously, not all books about children with special needs, disabilities, dysfunctions, or depression are as well written as others. There are fewer titles that take on these subjects, and therefore the recommendation process is dicey. Books of mediocre literary quality or that have not received star reviews may be included here. My criteria are: Is the story honest, realistic? Is it credible? Does it have valuable content and provide resolution? There is also my effort to maintain an objective viewpoint. I may not respond to a story with the same level of visceral connection as someone who is wrestling with a specific internal conflict. I've dismissed a story's merit only to have a student disagree. For instance, a young woman reacted to *The Reinvention of Edison Thomas* saying, "I really liked it. He reminded me of myself." I had no idea.

Many titles in *Remarkable Books about Young People with Special Needs* won't fit everyone. Some stories will feel tight, uncomfortably prickly, strange, and unfamiliar. Yet, there are revealing aspects in every story that fit us all. These selections are intended to lend courage, promote awareness, and share the enormity and fragility of being human. I hope that you'll boldly share some of these titles with your children, family, friends, faculty, students, and students' parents. Use some of these books in your classroom curriculum and talk about how it feels to be singled out, to be different, to be ignored, to be teased, or to be overlooked because you have a special need—that is, to be treated as though you're invisible. It is my hope that through sharing these stories, your readers—and all of us—reconsider the shortsightedness of "normal."

NOTES

1. Stephen Bartlett, "Bipolar Disorder behind Former Peru Superintendent's Departure," *Plattsburgh Press Republican,* October 16, 2011, http://pressrepublican.com/0100_news/x1548942417/Bipolar-disorder-behind-former-Peru-superintendents-departure.
2. William Gibson, *The Miracle Worker* (Scribner, 2008), 24.
3. Philip Schultz, "With Dyslexia, Words Failed Me and Then Saved Me," *New York Times,* September 4, 2011, www.nytimes.com/2011/09/04/opinion/sunday/with-dyslexia-words-failed-me-and-then-saved-me.html.

Index